Billy Hughes

*Prime Minister and Controversial
Founding Father of the Australian Labor Party*

ANEURIN HUGHES

WILEY

John Wiley & Sons Australia, Ltd

First published in 2005 by
John Wiley & Sons Australia, Ltd
42 McDougall Street, Milton Qld 4064

Offices also in Sydney and Melbourne

Typeset in 10.5/15.5 pt Caslon

© Aneurin Hughes 2005

National Library of Australia
Cataloguing-in-Publication data

Hughes, Aneurin.
  Billy Hughes: Prime Minister and controversial founding father of the Australian Labor Party.

  Includes index.
  ISBN-13   9 78174031 1366.
  ISBN-10   1 74031 136 1.

  1. Hughes, W. M. (William Morris), 1862–1952. 2. Australian Labor Party. 3. Prime ministers — Australia — Biography. 4. Australia — Politics and government — 1901–1945. I. Title.

994.04092

All rights reserved. Except as permitted under the *Australian Copyright Act 1968* (for example, a fair dealing for the purposes of study, research, criticism or review), no part of this book may be reproduced, stored in a retrieval system, communicated or transmitted in any form or by any means without prior written permission. All inquiries should be made to the publisher at the address above.

Photograph on cover and spine: by permission of the National Library of Australia
Author photo: Heide Smith Photography

Edited by Michael Wall

Printed in China by
Printplus Limited

10 9 8 7 6 5 4 3 2 1

For Elis and Sion

Contents

Acknowledgements vii
Introduction — Swagman to statesman ix

1. The early years 1
2. First brushes with the bush 11
3. Family strife and political life 25
4. 'Billy Bach' — the little Welshman 33
5. The slippery slope 43
6. Room at the top 53
7. Conscription and the birth of nationalism 63
8. The Peace Conference 75
9. Eclipsed but not extinguished 85
10. The frustrating years 97
11. Familial concerns 109
12. Back to the fray 119
13. Helen — a shadow fell 131
14. Grand old man 141
15. The peaceful aftermath 153

Notes 163
Bibliography 169
Index 171

Acknowledgements

My debts are numerous to the many who proffered good advice from spark of idea to ultimate product, but none greater than to Fred and Elizabeth Brenchley who encouraged me in every way, read several drafts, offered oodles of good sense and made numerous wise suggestions — all accompanied with liberal libations of splendid Margaret River white wine.

Thanks also to the staff of the National Library of Australia, particularly the stalwarts of the Manuscript Photographic and Newspaper sections, for unbridled help; my publishers John Wiley & Sons and editor Michael Wall for licking the text into shape; Bruce Adams and Stroudgate for continued support over the years; the University of Victoria and its previous Vice Chancellor, Professor Jarlath Ronayne; John Gage and the National Europe Centre at the ANU, as well as Professor R.V. Jackson for advice on relative money values. Many others have helped, including Ceris Gruffudd of the National Library of Wales; Murray and Menna Thomas of Llandudno; John Massey; Billy Hughes' great grandchildren, Diana Williams and David Hughes; Margot Davies, her mother Agnes and cousin Ken; Patricia Munro, daughter of Dorothy Mahomed; Dennis and Poppy Martin; and Stuart Rumshaw and ex-colleagues at the EU Delegation in Canberra.

Many others offered support or reminiscences relating to Billy — my apologies for not having the space to mention them all here.

The author and publisher would like to thank the following copyright holders, organisations and individuals for their permission to reproduce copyright material in this book.

All photographs except for Bryn Rosa and Dorothy Mahomed: by permission of the National Library of Australia; Bryn Rosa: Aneurin Hughes; Dorothy Mahomed: reproduced with permission of Patricia Munro.

Every effort has been made to trace the ownership of copyright material. Information that will enable the publisher to rectify any error or omission in subsequent editions will be welcome. In such cases, please contact the Permissions Section of John Wiley & Sons Australia, Ltd, who will arrange for the payment of the usual fee.

INTRODUCTION

Swagman to statesman

Despite considerable literature devoted to him, some of it furnished by himself, Billy Hughes remains a will-of-the-wisp though iconic figure in recent Australian history. My interest in him percolated slowly during my six years as the European Union's Ambassador to Australia and New Zealand from 1995 to 2002. I lived near a suburb in Canberra named after him and, nearly 50 years after his death, radio and television programs were still made about him. Sons and grandsons were named after him, such as Australia's one-time cricket captain Bill Laurie. His name still appears regularly in newspaper articles comparing contemporary issues to those he had to contend with: his belligerence as prime minister during World War I, and the behaviour of today's bellicose statesmen; his opposition to the arrival of Maltese 'boat people', and the Australian Government's position over the Tampa affair and refugee policy; Hughes' and John Howard's nursing of the 'Little Digger' image; his belief in the White Australia Policy, and the rise and fall of Pauline Hanson. Budding leaders of the current Australian Labor Party have still talked of him in terms of 'King Rat' for splitting the party in 1917 over conscription. For Gough Whitlam, Hughes had 'dealt three disastrous blows to the Labor Party: he split the Party, he so polarised the elements which remained in it that factionalism became almost an addiction and he undermined the Labor Party's trust in the very concept of leadership'. Some academics think he poisoned Australia's relations with Asia with his fervent defence of the White Australia Policy and refusal to allow a racial equality clause to be inserted in the Versailles Treaty,[1] while others maintain that Hughes' position in demanding maximum reparations from Germany after World War I was immoral and possibly contributed to the rise of the Third Reich.

Billy Hughes

Other commentators have argued that his refusal at the Paris Peace Conference to allow Japan to exercise mandatory powers over the Pacific islands south of the equator saved Australia from invasion in World War II, others that he was the progenitor of an authentic Australian foreign policy, and one of the first real Australian nationalists. The poet Mary Gilmore, for example, wrote to him: 'You made Australia articulate, and gave her identity in Europe which at that time saw her as neither.' She also once recorded Hughes standing at the door of Parliament House saying, 'Tell them fellers to stop their gab. Only wise men talk here.' And then he talked for an hour, 'but even a pin couldn't drop lest a word be lost'. Gerard Henderson wrote of him in the *Sydney Morning Herald* as 'the most influential political leader in Australian history. So far Billy Hughes (despite his many faults) has been the only Prime Minister willing to put guns before butter.'

Observers described him variously as: 'a bundle of common sense'; 'storm bird of Australian politics'; 'an alley cat scraggy, acute and resilient'; at times 'charming and witty' but more usually 'cantankerous, mocking and bullying'; 'like Fluellen, a truculent jester'; 'a curious combination of candour and secretiveness, small, narrow-shouldered and stooped though strong handed with big bony knuckles, his face pinched and seamed, his accent, working class London but with a slight intonation of Wales'. Above all, 'He was too deaf to listen, too loud to ignore, and too small to hit'.[2] 'Conflict', he once said, 'was the breath of existence' and again, 'Life is conflict seasoned by endurance'.

For Sir Ronald Mungo-Ferguson, governor-general when Hughes became Prime Minister, later Lord Novar: 'He had all the arts of a crab, when he does not wish to be drawn he withdraws within the impenetrable shell of his designs... always dauntless, cheery... his dash and genius lend charm to a wild career... he does not know how to devolve responsibility and is too often unable to grapple with detail.' And for me, he was of Welsh extraction, claimed to speak Welsh, was consistently proud of his Celtic heritage, and had the same name as my father, though in fact not related to our family.

Having read most, if not all, the books by or about him; waded through the 33 metres of material left to the National Library of Australia (NLA) by his widow (including a somewhat disconcerting volume 50 consisting of a pair of his false teeth and his hearing aid); perused the data gathered by the Australian Dictionary of Biography; and chased references in the National Archives, state libraries and Hansard, for me the intriguing discovery was that there was so little which emerged about William Morris Hughes *the person*. Lawrence Fitzhardinge[3] described his two-volume biography as a 'political biography' — more about Hughes the politician than the man. Donald Horne's more recent acidulous offerings[4] are hardly biographies, being written from a pronounced partisan perspective — Horne describes them as a 'portrait'. Farmer Whyte's earlier biography,[5] although not a hagiography, is crisper, not very accurate and somewhat gentle on Hughes' faults. Hughes himself, while amassing a vast quantity of papers at his Lindfield home and constituency office, includes meagre glimpses of himself and his personal relations with family and friends, and there are only the most vague references to his life prior to his emergence as an elected politician, other than his two volumes of reminiscences. Following his marriage to Mary Campbell, according to Manning Clark, 'He was no longer a man with a private face, only a public one'.[6]

Hughes' reminiscences were written when he was well into his eighties. For one who was so meticulous in keeping the most minute scraps of memorabilia, handwritten notes, speeches and newspaper articles, the absence of any significant intimate early records — from his years prior to coming to Australia, his two years roughing it in Queensland, his early days in Sydney and his first family — must have been deliberate. His records, though voluminous, suggest conscious weeding and selectivity. In the 50 volumes of papers held by the NLA there are very few examples that cast Hughes in a bad light, significant gaps in the correspondence, and evidence of attempts to disguise facts such as his occasional use of shorthand. He knew that his accumulation of documents would be examined by posterity, and posterity would have only what he wanted it to have.

Billy Hughes

However, there are enough titbits of revelation to whet one's appetite for more, and even to tantalise. From looking at family letters, financial records, congratulatory telegrams, birthday and Christmas cards, household bills and trivia, and talks with some of his descendants and others still alive who knew him personally, what emerges is a picture of a man much more complex and perhaps more interesting than the rather stilted and cardboard caricature often described. Looking at photographs of him and his contemporaries, it is easy to fall into the trap of condescension and superiority from seeing the dress people wore in his times: the Zapata moustaches affected by most men; the variety of beards; the high, stiff collars and frockcoats; and the stilted language and biblical cadences employed. Of Hughes there are sufficient hints to suggest character traits in seeming contradiction to that recorded of the public man.

Hughes is infamous for having had more than 100 secretaries, but he had been in the Federal Parliament for over 50 years, longer than anyone else in any democratic legislature (except for a Charles Villiers, who represented Wolverhampton in the British Parliament for 63 years), and even in those days he did on occasion need to employ three secretaries at the same time to deal with correspondence of more than 600 letters a week.

He could not suffer fools at all, let alone gladly, but could inspire the intense devotion of Pat Romans, who was his secretary for over 10 years until August 1944 and would not hear a word against him. Of her relationship with Hughes, Tom Hungerford, one of his press secretaries, wrote that he was, 'As cold as sea-ice, vain as a peacock, cruel as a butcher bird, sly as a weasel and mean as cat shit, yet there was in him something that bound that gentle and most competent woman to his chariot wheel throughout the vicissitudes of his long decline'. Hungerford lasted three weeks and wrote to Hughes, 'I will never work for you again. I'd rather go to bed with a sabre-toothed tiger.' Another of his secretaries, Barbara Rogers, lamented having to leave him to look after her father, 'as I have enjoyed working with such a great man … I have liked your manner (abrupt at times) enjoyed your wise-cracking …'. One secretary, named Howe, remained with him for five years, from 1925 to 1930, and became a friend for life. His masseur, Bachli, who would almost have to unwind him when he got up in the mornings, stayed with him for 30 years despite being regularly sacked, eventually resigning over a disagreement in 1949. John Lloyd (first cousin to Ned Kelly) stayed with Hughes for 20 years.

On the other hand, people like Morris West the author and Jack Fingleton the cricketer, who also worked for him, remained only for a short time. West became secretary to Hughes in 1943: 'What I didn't know was that I was one of a long line of secretaries, which at that time numbered 72. The old man would in furious anger sweep his desk clear of papers and say: "pick them up". I lasted three months.' Fingleton, who lasted much longer until he resigned on 9 July 1943, found him completely impossible, once opining that Larwood, the English fast bowler who struck terror in many a batsman, was a 'novice compared with Billy Hughes'.

What was necessary in dealing with him was simply not to kow-tow to his tantrums; if you were prepared to act as a doormat, Hughes would stomp all over you. A new secretary Hughes found in his office one day was lambasted for putting his papers in a particular place. 'Why the hell did you put them there?' raged Hughes. 'Because you told me to put them there', said the young man. 'I'll be buggered if I did', said Hughes. 'And I'll be buggered if you didn't', said the lad. Hughes looked at his hearing aid and said, 'Would you mind repeating that?'. The new secretary did so, slowly and exactly. Hughes scratched his nose and said, 'Well if you say it like that I suppose I did'.[7] And there was no new secretary for some time. Another who lasted longer than most was one Keith Waller (later Sir Keith), known as 'Spats', who also had the gumption to give Hughes as good as he got. Hughes said to him on his first day, 'It's really very simple. The others all agree that everything is my fault. I say it's theirs. You, Waller, are uniquely placed to find out which of us is right.' The young man stayed with Hughes longer than most secretaries and parted on being promoted, with goodwill on both sides.[8] Of his many secretaries he once said to journalists: 'They say I eat my secretaries. It's a lie. I'm on a strict medical diet.'

He could provoke his opponents to apoplexy and engender both disdain and even hatred but also command intense loyalty, even adulation, from colleagues and friends. He could be exceedingly mean-spirited, petty and vindictive, as when he physically evicted a farmer, a certain Bellinger, and his family from land he owned. On another occasion, during a whistle-stop tour arguing the need for conscription, he chastised the Queensland police for failing to take action against a protester who had thrown a rotten egg at him when he was addressing a crowd at Warwick on 29 November 1917. The police sergeant in question defended his refusal to take summary action on the grounds that he was obliged only to recognise the laws of Queensland not the Commonwealth, but had demanded of the crowd a fair go for the PM. Hughes took the matter up with the then Premier of Queensland, Thomas Joseph Ryan, no friend of the Prime Minister but a wily and effective political operator who skilfully steered a diplomatic course through the troubled waters Hughes had fomented. In the subsequent court hearing, testimony was given by a Constable Dufficey who had been present during the fracas. The outcome was that Patrick Brosnan, who had thrown the well-directed missile, was charged with creating a disturbance and fined £1, but he was not charged with having thrown the egg since in the view of the police, although they had found three eggs in Brosnan's pocket this was not evidence that he had been the thrower. As a result, Hughes moved to set up the Commonwealth Police Force and was mocked by the Labor leader Frank Anstey who in Parliament said: 'We have seen how from a little acorn the oak tree grows. By God! Out of a rotten egg they manufactured the Federal Police.'

However, Hughes could also demonstrate generosity of spirit, compassion and self-deprecation. To a long-suffering portrait painter who, having tried with might and main to keep the great man sitting still for him, expostulated that he could in no way do Hughes justice unless he stopped constantly fidgeting, Hughes replied gloomily, 'It's not justice I want, it's mercy'.[9] *The Times* of London wrote in its obituary of him: 'His personality contained strange contradictions.' One gets the overriding impression of a gadfly or butterfly flitting hither and thither revealing only occasional facets of a multilayered persona, sufficient to confirm the casual observer's prejudices in his regard. He was like Gwydion, a very early figure in Welsh mythology, half-human, half-spirit, who could change his nature, form and substance at will to suit whatever circumstances prevailed.

What follows, then, is not another biography, nor is there any strict chronological coherence. Some of the major domestic and international issues he was intimately involved in are referred to, as well as some of the stories which helped construct the legend. Yet in trying to draw out more the man than the politician, the focus is on matters such as his relations with the members of his families; his health, particularly his deafness and chronic dyspepsia; and his virtues and his vices. What we find is a man with one foot firmly anchored in the nineteenth century and the other very much in the twentieth; an Empire loyalist and imperialist, but ardent Australian nationalist; a man who, despite his peregrinations through Australia's political landscape, would always maintain that he stood for the common man, but accepted a Companion of Honour (though refusing a knighthood and a seat in the House of Lords); one who was a firm believer in the vocation of the English-speaking peoples yet spoke French, kept learning Italian, and had some Latin, Greek and Welsh; a man who preached the virtues of family but had six children with a lady he never married. It is a story of a Welsh larrikin born a cockney; it is an Australian odyssey from log cabin to white house, from swagman to statesman.

Chapter 1

The early years

Much has been written of Billy Hughes' political career from the time he first began to exhibit both his vigour and organisational skills in the early labour and trade union movements in Sydney. However, there is little real content regarding his formative years in Wales and London — much anecdote but not much substance. Some light is shed by piecing together fragments in frequent letters from Welsh people claiming kinship and old friends from his London days recording a past memory or recollection. These fragments litter his accumulated papers from the time, one suspects, that he first had some secretarial support until his latter days when he had outlived most of his contemporaries.

Albeit lauded in Wales as the only Welshman other than Lloyd George to have become a prime minister, Hughes was actually born in Pimlico, London, at 7 Moreton Place, the son of William and Jane Hughes, née Morris. His mother, the daughter of Peter and Mary Morris of Winllan Farm in Llansantffraid Powys Wales, was 37 years old when she married and was in service in London when she met her husband. She did not speak Welsh and was an Anglican. When Billy was seven years old she died at Glasbury on her way to visit her parents and he was sent to live with his father's sister, Mary Hughes, who kept an apartment house in Llandudno in North Wales. (Wales is speckled with towns beginning with 'Llan' — an old Welsh word meaning 'church'.) Llandudno — the church of Saint Tudno — was a holiday resort much favoured in Victorian times both by reasonably well-to-do English visitors and workers from the cotton mills of Lancashire and Yorkshire. Though wearing a patina of seeming English gentility, the town's heartbeat was Welsh and the neighbouring countryside is still predominantly Welsh speaking. Towering over the town is the gloomy presence of the Great Orme, a slab of limestone rock rising from the Menai Straits, deriving its name from the Norwegian word for worm or sea serpent — a linguistic heritage dating from the Viking raids along the coast in the eighth century. For the Welsh, the Orme has always been a place of mystery and romance.

What his father had to say on Billy's removal from London to Llandudno is uncertain, as precious little is known of Hughes père. (A French newspaper, in an article on Billy Hughes, said that his father had worked on the construction of the Palace of Westminster,[1] and his profession was reported variously as being that of a master moulder engaged in the construction of the House of Commons, and carpenter and joiner in the House of Lords.[2] He was known also to be a deacon in his local church. Otherwise, the record is scant.) It was often the case in Wales, though, that a child who had lost their mother would be sent to live with relations, since most fathers in those days worked such excessively long hours that earning a living and rearing an infant were incompatible. Moreover, there are no indications that the Hughes had any relatives, or even close friends, in London who might have been able to take the boy.

Schooldays in Wales

Billy's aunt Mary lived at 16 Abbey Road, Bryn Rosa, at the top of the town not far from Gwddaeth Terrace where his mother had also lived at one time. Among his aunt's regular clients was John Bright, one of the leading members of the Anti Corn Law League, one time member of Parliament successively for Durham, Manchester and Birmingham, and fervent opponent of the Crimean War, who always dressed in broadcloth and Quaker hat. He undoubtedly had an influence on the young Billy, and many years later was quoted in Hughes' first major speech in the New South Wales Parliament. Hughes stayed with his aunt from 1868 to 1873 and began his education at Mclaughlin's School in Bodlondeb Hill before going to Llandudno Grammar School in Cwlach Street. His first school subsequently became a Welsh Wesleyan chapel, and a tablet on the wall records Hughes' attendance in its previous incarnation. At the school he was fortunate to have as headmaster Dr George Roberts, one of Wales' foremost and most revered educators of the day, but who was a stickler for discipline and, according to Hughes, was an artiste at wielding the cane.

Here, among other things, he learnt fisticuffs, swimming and seamanship, became a speedy runner and was remembered as the school marbles champion, storing his won marbles in a hole on the slopes of the Great Orme behind his house. Dr Roberts, whatever else he thought of Hughes, was a harsh critic of his handwriting, which showed little improvement over the years. Billy's closest friend in Llandudno was a certain William Henderson; other friends included Archie and Willie Van Gelder, Fred and Sam Jackson, Eddie and Johnny Ridge, and George Brookes — all names Hughes remembered during a visit to Llandudno in May 1916.[3]

His years at Llandudno were happy ones and the various references to the town in his papers are always positive: anyone writing to him claiming acquaintance with the place received a warm reply. His papers include a ticket issued by the Llandudno Urban District Council during his visit there in 1932: 'To W.M. Hughes Marine Drive. This ticket permits free use of the Marine Drive to and from the Great Orme Cemeteries only. 18 August 1932.' There is also a letter from a Mr Barwell who had previously been music master at Llandudno Grammar School and also organist and choirmaster at Holy Trinity Church when Hughes was in the choir. He wrote that Billy had received his first wage — a half crown, representing one month's pay — for his efforts in the church choir. Another letter on his 77th birthday conjured up a very Victorian scene which could have been replicated in many seaside resorts of the era, referring to the delights of Llandudno: 'The minstrel show in Happy Valley, the steamer "La Marguerite" leaving for Bangor and the Menai Straits, a walk through Bodafon Woods, the cable car climbing the steep hill, and invalids being wheeled along the promenade in their bath chairs.'

3

Billy Hughes

He spent all his holidays from school in Llandudno with his mother's family at the Plas Bedw farm where his grandparents lived, and the nearby Winllan Cottage (also known as Aunty Mason's Cottage) in Llansantffraid. He wrote that the family were a trifle unusual, and, although they belonged to a strict Calvinistic sect, his maiden aunt Elizabeth was designated as the family representative to attend the local Anglican church. His uncle Peter, with whom he shared a bedroom, would periodically go on a drunken bender and then swear to eschew the demon drink for evermore, filled with remorse. According to Hughes, the farm had been in the Morris family for 500 years. Llansantffraid lies six miles from the border with England and is one of a number of small rural towns and villages in a gentle countryside of rolling hills and valleys where numerous relations of the Morrises lived.

This is typical border country where farms frequently have some fields in England and some in Wales, and where the children of the area often have different national loyalties, some supporting the Red Dragon, others the Red Rose. Hughes would have imbibed much of this border culture. On one hand was the romanticism of the Celtic world, its long history, heroics and stoicism through Roman occupation, Viking incursions and Saxon invasion. On the other hand he would have been affected by the deep conservatism and respect for traditional values of a pastoral community that delighted in tracing its husbandry of the land back for generations. This duality remained with him throughout his life: a high regard for individual self-reliance and a stoic acceptance of 'the slings and arrows of outrageous fortune' but also reverence for norms of civilised behaviour, the necessary underpinning of a democratic state.

These traits would also have been deepened both by his personal experience — in losing his mother at an early age and being sent away to live with someone he probably had never previously met — and by the prevailing sentiments of the day, with Britain at the height of her imperial might and glory.

In an extant passport and other records, such as his entry in the 1945 edition of *Who's Important in Government*, Hughes gave his birthplace as Wales, yet in his draft for the 1944 edition of the *Encyclopedia of the World* he corrected 'born in Wales' to 'born in London', although a reference to Llandudno as his birthplace was not corrected. As for his birth date he was consistent in recording it as 25 September 1864, but Fitzhardinge, checking his birth certificate, noted that it was two years earlier. Percy Deane, who was closer to Hughes than most, once raised the discrepancy in the dates of his birth with him, to be blasted with a 'Gahd, blithering blanky blazes wasn't I there when I was born?'. The NLA has on file one of his passports[4] in which his birth details, wrongly, are given as Wales, 25 September 1864, and his height is noted as 5 foot 5 inches and his hair grey.

We know much more about the family on the maternal side than the paternal, so it is surprising that there is no trace of any personal view of his mother or what his private feelings were in her regard. However, in the little Llansantffraid parish church there is a four-light window depicting the arms of the Australian states and carrying the inscription: 'Dedicated to the glory of God and in memory of his mother Jane Hughes a native of this parish by the Right Honourable William Morris Hughes Prime Minister of the Commonwealth of Australia 1921.' One of the few references to his father came in a letter of 5 August 1947 noting that Hughes senior hailed from Holyhead in Anglesey, although the family may originally have come from the Vale of Clwyd: 'He and his brothers and sisters — there were at least six in the family and all born and raised in Holyhead.'

Within the sound of Bow Bells

After more than five years of living with his aunt in North Wales, the nearly 12-year-old Billy returned to London. We do not know whether the return was planned or precipitate: he appears to have been happy at his Llandudno school and at Winllan farm with his mother's family, and one wonders why he left still at a comparatively tender age. Fitzhardinge suggests that this was to move on to secondary education, but he could have done this in Llandudno; had his aunt perhaps had enough of him? Had she died? There is no evidence of his father visiting him in Llandudno and we do not know whether on return to London he went to live with his father or not. This lacuna in the story of Hughes' early years is at one level puzzling but also typical: puzzling since Fitzhardinge spent many, many hours quizzing Hughes for his book, in Canberra and in Sydney, such that one would have expected to read much more of Hughes' early relationships with family and friends; and yet typical of Hughes propensity for keeping in the recesses of his memory those elements in his story that were either distasteful or painful, or impugned the image of himself he wanted to impart.

We do know that he did not return to his father's house at Moreton Place[5] and that he went instead to live in Ponsonby Terrace, Vauxhall, in lodgings, according to Fitzhardinge. Cockneys are traditionally defined as those Londoners born within the sound of Bow's church bells and Hughes could claim to be one of that ilk both by virtue of where he had been born and where he received the bulk of his secondary education. He began his London schooling in 1874 at St Stephen's Church of England school in Rochester Row, Pimlico, Westminster. The school had been founded in 1846 by a lady who had married into the Coutts Banking family, Baroness Burdett Coutts, the daughter of a radical Member of Parliament, Sir Francis Burdett, whose benefactions included aid to Aboriginal communities in Australia and endowment of the bishopric of Adelaide.

The school seems to have been variously called St Stephen's and Burdett-Coutts. It acquired the St Stephen's tag when the church was built alongside. The area was known for many years as the Devil's Acre and was regarded as one of the filthiest slums in London. Supported by her friend Charles Dickens, the Baroness had persuaded the Dean and Chapter of Westminster to give her this tract of land, an awful place of open sewers and louse ridden tenements 'which housed every kind of criminal' to see what could be done to alleviate the appalling conditions in which so many lived.

Hughes clearly had fond memories of the school and his days there, although in a talk to boys at the school during his visit in 1916 he recalled his first classroom of 40 young lads: 'the room ill-lit by gas, terrible ventilation, a black hole of Calcutta, the windows — mere slits'. A close schoolboy friend at St Stephen's, J.S. Hairgill, wrote that they used to march out of school to the tune of 'Let the Hills Resound with Song'. Much later in a letter to the Salvation Army's newspaper *The War Cry*, Hughes gave his favourite hymn as being 'Abide With Me', one of the hymns sung at his funeral. He recalled the 'dear old vicar Mr Tennent and the times I used to take a turn in ringing the bells in the Church'.

He was only 14 when he began a five-year apprenticeship as a student teacher at St Stephen's. School records describe him as short and spare, with long spindly legs, and tough as whipcord. They also show, among other things, that he successfully passed the fifth standard in 1875 and sixth standard in 1876, and that he won a prize in geometry in 1875 and a certificate of proficiency in model drawing in 1877. On 9 March the following year, Baroness Coutts herself presented him with the prize in a competitive examination: *The International Political Classical and Historical Atlas*. Allegedly he was also given a prize for French by Lord Harrowley and presented with a volume of Shakespeare's plays by Matthew Arnold. (It is possible that a chord was struck between the young scholar and Arnold on the latter learning that Hughes' previous schooling had been in Llandudno, which Arnold had visited in 1865 and had written of the view to the west from above the town: 'the eternal softness and mild light of the west, the low line of the mystic Anglesey and the precipitous Penmaenmawr'.) At some point in his time at the school Hughes became a volunteer with the Royal Fusiliers.

An independent young man

The school embodied both discipline and wide learning, with Hughes drinking deeply of the educational draughts on offer and immersing himself especially in the classics of literature. He was also manifestly well versed in the Bible; in his previous London days he had been taken on most Sundays to the Welsh Baptist Chapel in Moorfield where his father was a deacon, although he was christened in St Margaret's Anglican Church, Westminster, by a then famous Dean, Arthur Penrhyn Stanley. Both influences are evident in his political career, particularly in his speeches and the metaphors and quotations he employed; on one occasion a newspaper devoted several column inches analysing his Biblical imagery, which resonated with his contemporaries but would have left a younger and less widely read audience somewhat nonplussed.

Around this time it was, though the record is unclear, that he left the school and began thinking of taking the long journey to Australia. One is left to wonder at the relationship between Hughes and his father. Could it have been estrangement from his father that launched him towards Australia? There is hardly a trace of his father in Hughes' papers, no recollections, no anecdotes and not the slightest trace of letters back home or letters from home, no mention of anything left to him by his father (he was, after all, an only child). Moreover, the father had barely known the child after the age of seven, so relations between them could never have been particularly close. It may have been that the father remarried or that the young Hughes carried a bitter resentment at what he might have regarded as being abandoned as unwanted baggage. Or maybe his father, the Baptist deacon, was a stickler for the ordinances of his faith such that young Billy rebelled and decided even so young that he had no choice other than to go his own way and carve his own destiny.

Perhaps it was that there was nothing to hold him in Britain. There is little evidence of him having forged any close friendships during his teenage years other than with the Payne family, who were neighbours and with whom he corresponded irregularly for a long period after his arrival in Australia and visited during his first trip back to Britain in 1907 (the date of his father's death is not recorded, but had occurred before this in 1907). He gave differing reasons for his decision to head for the Antipodes: his love of travel, or the romance of seeing with his friend George Payne the tall ships in London's East India docks bound

The early years

for the great south land, spurring his fancy. Another account has him sitting on a stool in Coutts Bank in London being thoroughly dispirited by the elderly clerks there present with bald heads bowed, and then walking out down Cockspur Street and in the nearby shipping offices, seeing a notice concerning migrant passages to Australia for £5, taking a coin from his pocket and saying, 'Heads Australia, Tails Coutts Bank'.[6]

Chapter 2

First brushes with the bush

In October 1884, George Payne and his father drove Hughes in a little pony cart to Blackwall Pier to join the steamboat to Gravesend, the first leg of the great adventure of sailing to Australia. In London Docks, he boarded the good ship *Duke of Westminster* for a voyage that was to last two months. The ship's manifest, held at the Queensland State Library, notes his presence aboard as an 'assisted immigrant', and also records all passengers and what class they were travelling in: 480 in steerage, 11 in first class. Hughes was most definitely in steerage.

The picture of his early days in both Queensland and Sydney is similar to his Welsh and London background for its paucity of detail. The history of his first two years in Australia has been usually regarded as more literary than literate, especially since there is little corroborative evidence for Hughes' version of events. However, by piecing together clues in letters to him and contemporary reminiscences by others who had no interest in creating legend, there emerges a rough idea of his journeyings and the rigours of that period.

What we have are his reflections gathered in tranquillity and the reminiscences of numerous colleagues and acquaintances. In those days before radio and television the 'gift of the gab' was not to be disparaged, and the teller of good yarns was someone to treasure. Storytelling flourished almost as an artform as settlers gathered around their fires in the bush, squatters in their homesteads or in pubs or clubs in the towns and cities. Tall tales there were aplenty and many an Australian Munchausen flourished. In this regard, Hughes was exceptional, demonstrating early on his capacity not only to relate an interesting account of his experiences but garnish and embellish them with colourful language, humour and dramatic imagery. Throughout the literature about him, stories told by him are frequently quoted, and letters to him from old comrades or diggers drag his memory back to particular incidents. Most Australians over 50 will remember an older relative telling them some tale about 'Billy'. In his own reminiscences, biographical books and material the dressing up of his experiences is evident. The *Sunday Herald* wrote of him cultivating his own legend and 'being capable of inspiring fanatical devotion and violent antipathy'. Hughes himself provided much of the content in the biographies by Farmer Whyte and Fitzhardinge so that, beyond what is attested in the public record, it is a challenging task to distinguish the hard core of fact in many accounts of his exploits from the persiflage and padding.

A swagman's life

When he landed in Brisbane on 8 December 1884 the times were not auspicious: he maintained he broke his ankle in a fall on the day of his arrival and, though recording that he had obtained his first job as 'boots' in a Brisbane hotel, work in the city was hard to find. Moving on soon to try his luck in the hinterland he found that prospects were not greatly improved, with the Queensland countryside in the grip of a severe drought. His sojourn over the next two years saw him doing an array of different labouring jobs to ensure a 'feed': he picked pineapples for 14 hours a day, for which he received 10 shillings a week, and became a navvy breaking stones on the Mitchell-to-Charleville railway construction line. At Mitchell he worked at the Railway Goods shed for Messrs White, Reid and Roseman. He tramped, with a companion named William Fox, over the Mitchell Plains where there was 'not a tree to be seen, nothing but sand'. With another fellow swagman he embarked on a long trek from Adamvale to Brisbane, some 600 miles away — a journey which took them four months and during which they were lucky to survive the rigours of the bush.

He worked as a stockman driving cattle overland and as a boundary rider and posthole digger before becoming a volunteer private in the Queensland Defence Forces, being assigned to guard a coal hulk at Thursday Island in the northern tip of the state. According to Browne, this was to combat a feared Russian invasion. He acted as cook for timber cutters in the forest 'humping his bluey' (carrying his pack on his back). At Roma he worked in a blacksmith's shop, tramped on to Bassett's vineyard to pick grapes, then on to Maryborough, where Fred Payne (brother of Hughes' friend George Payne in London)[1] had ended up, and then to the Gympie gold rush. He also worked at Bowen, and later as a steward on coastal ships heading to Cooktown and the Gulf with the ASN Company. He trailed after sheep along the overland stock routes from Peak Downs across western Queensland to Hillston and Bourke in New South Wales, much of the time on horseback or in a sulky.

At Orange he worked with a farmer called Sweeney bagging potatoes. The farmer's wife was Irish and spoke to him in Irish, he replying in Welsh and understanding only two words out of fifty.[2] He acted as a shearer's offsider, binding the cut sheaves for 4 shillings a day and maintained this had been the most back-breaking job he had ever undertaken. According to Sladen,[3] it was during the early days in Queensland spending 15 months on the hot plains and driving sheep into the mountains of New South Wales that he caught the cold that contributed to the deafness from which he suffered all his life. In the *L'Information* article of 20 April 1919, Hughes said he lost complete hearing in one ear. The *Herald* of 2 February 1923 wrote that his deafness was the result of a severe illness in the public hospital in Orange following a chill contracted on the roads. However, the Reverend Mowll, in his funeral oration for Hughes, said that he became deaf while at sea through a drenching he had received.

Billy Hughes

Jack of all trades

Hughes described arriving in Sydney on the good ship *Maranoa*: 'For two years I had been a wanderer in the North and Western Queensland. Since it was May it was freezing — no shirt, a flannel, a thin black alpaca coat, light canvas pants, shoes and socks that had seen better days and a black felt hat with a broad brim.' He had half a crown in his pocket — wages for three weeks' work in the galley of the *Maranoa*. Landing in Sydney he saw a sign 'Wanted: a pantry man' and took the job at 10 shillings a week plus board, calling himself 'Bill'. On the second day his duties were doubled but the wages remained the same — a practice known in the common parlance of the time as an 'Irishman's raise'. The next week he left for a job at The Golden Gate for 15 shillings per week. He worked in various other Sydney restaurants, and in one recollection said that he had also worked as an oven-maker.

Sometime in 1887 he moved into a lodging house in Flinders Street, Moore Park, paying 5 shillings a week and spending 7/6 per week on food and clothing. Not long afterwards he married his landlady's daughter, Elizabeth Cutts, according to Fitzhardinge, though he was unable to establish the date of the marriage; successive Parliamentary Handbooks recorded the marriage date as 1886. Farmer Whyte, who would seem to have obtained his information from Arthur Hughes, Hughes' step-son, also wrote that a marriage had taken place but that it was in Melbourne in 1884 or 1885. This was evidentially not the case: at this stage Hughes had never visited Melbourne and did not arrive in Sydney until May 1887. In 1940, Buchanan, in an unpublished book on Australian prime ministers, wrote that the marriage had taken place in Queensland two years after Hughes had arrived in Australia. In the Coronation issue of Burke's Peerage of 1938 Hughes is recorded as having married in 1886, a date which would seem to have been sent them by Hughes himself. Browne also wrote that Hughes had married but in 1890 and that his immersion in politics became the source of such domestic discontent that his home life became more and more unhappy.

There is no record of Hughes himself ever clarifying the circumstances of his relationship with Elizabeth. We know, however, that by 1890 he had settled in Balmain in Palmer Street with Elizabeth and indeed with two children: Arthur, Elizabeth's son from a previous liaison, and Ethel, their first daughter.[4]

Finding his voice

Shortly afterwards he bought a shop for 30 shillings in Beattie Street, a working-class area of wharf labourers, coal lumpers and the unemployed. Here he repaired locks, mended umbrellas, ground knives, sold secondhand books and tobacco, and conducted a debating society in an upstairs room over the shop. Also in Beattie Street was Dick's Hotel, where supporters of the early labour movement and members of embryonic trade unions met. Money, however, was a problem and the meagre pickings from the shop had to be supplemented by Elizabeth's earnings as a skivvy: washing, cleaning and ironing. Hughes, too, sought whatever extra work could provide the family with the means of sustenance, once even acting as a soldier in a production by George Rignold of Shakespeare's *Henry V* at Sydney's old Her Majesty's Theatre. He was to receive 12/6 per week for 150 performances; in the event the play ran for only three weeks. Bumping into Hughes many years later, Rignold looked at him and said: 'Haven't we met before?' 'Yes', replied Hughes 'on the fields of Agincourt'. Sir Robert Garran, a friend of Hughes and one-time attorney-general, recorded that probably the first time he saw Hughes was in that production, as a soldier in Henry's army.[5]

Hughes is said to have given one of his first public speeches at the first Eisteddfod to be held in Sydney, in 1890, for which he received a prize of a guinea and a blue ribbon to be draped around his shoulders.[6] The adjudicator in Sydney was a Russell Evans and the prize was presented to Hughes by Sir Henry Parkes, the then premier of NSW. It was for an impromptu speech, the theme to be chosen by the contending speakers themselves; Hughes' choice of theme was, iconoclastically, 'Myself'. Strongly influenced by Henry George, the American socialist proselytiser and ardent advocate of free trade and a single tax on land, Hughes' nascent radicalism was fired and his political course begun. He remembered sitting in the old Protestant Hall listening spellbound to George, of whom he later said, 'What a wonderful man he was'.

The 1890s witnessed the worst depression Australia has ever known, with the crash of the price of wool, and land values sky-high and, in 1891, what was called the Maritime Strike, though it involved much more than seamen and was perhaps the most bitter labour struggle in Australia's history. Hughes took part in the strike but was not a strike leader and argued that the men should settle: 'What about your wives and children. Are you going to let them starve? You cannot win.' Such a view was not popular: the strike lasted two months and led to the establishment of the Labour Electoral League, of which Hughes was an early member. The *Australian Magazine*, which covered the strike, wrote of 'an element of grotesquerie in the frail form of this little man stooping forward until he reduces his own height by inches ... speaking for the wharfies six foot high who could throw him into the sea and sailors who could stow him in their hip pockets. But he stood, restraining them from going too far, his influence, his moderating advice, his keen sighted appreciation ... that steadied the movement when the movement mostly needed steadying.' Though regarded as a fiery militant by his political enemies, Hughes thought strikes to be the last and worst of options; what was important was negotiation and arbitration, and in this latter regard Hughes may have been influenced by Henry Richards, a fellow Welshman known in Wales as 'the apostle of peace' and author of the first bill ever passed by the House of Commons on 9 July 1873 in favour of a general and permanent system of arbitration.

The troubled decade saw many spirits crushed, such as Hughes' friend William Lane, who sailed away in July 1893 in pursuit of a dream to create a socialistic state in Paraguay. Hughes' earliest foray into union affairs followed and he became political organiser for the Trade Council in Young in the same year. In 1899, he was appointed the secretary of the Wharf Labourers Union. An erstwhile colleague, Ted Hillyer, recalled in a letter to Hughes how the wharfside union came into being:

> You happened along to the quay and spoke to four of the labourers, one of them saw me standing in George Street opposite the lavatory, he left the company and came up to me and said: 'Ted, Mr Hughes is speaking about starting a union on the water front ...' That was where it all began ...

As late as 1942 Hillyer was still corresponding, reminding Hughes of the meetings at the old school rooms in Church Hill.

Not only did he organise the wharf labourers who had been scattered in the aftermath of the 1890s strike, he established them once more as a power in the land; he had their pay increased and their hours reduced, and became their general secretary for over 20 years. By 1899, the union was the most powerful metropolitan trade organisation in the country. He also set up the Trolly, Draymen and Carters Union, the Waterside Workers Federation and the Transport Workers Federation. Hughes maintained that when secretary of the Waterside Union he never received a penny in salary, not even for personal expenses during the whole period of his tenure of office. *Punch* of 3 December 1908 wrote that 'the waterside workers are the roughest, the fiercest, the most lawless body of workmen in the Commonwealth' and that Hughes had done for them what William Guthrie Spence, 'the prince of labour organisers', had done for the shearers. The shearers' union was the strongest in the land and became the Australian Workers Union. Union politics became an obsession for Hughes. He was described as 'a firefly all over the place, spare agile frame, steely grey-blue eyes, domineering at times', using 'language full of idiomatic piquancy'.

An article in the *Sydney Sunday Times* in 1920 carried a photograph of Hughes' shop in Balmain and reported that it was in the old Unity Hall in Balmain where he practised his oratorical skills. Each evening he would dash down the street to get a can of kerosene from one Bill Mahoney, later to become the federal member for Dalley. The kerosene provided light for meetings with fellow socialists and trade unionists from 8.00 pm onwards and, when the meetings finished, allowed him to read his law books in the flickering flame. Not all comments were adulatory: T.W. McCristal, in his dramatically titled book *Sensational Exposure of W.M. Hughes*, wrote 'when he came among the wharfies ... his toes were poking out of his boots, and the tail of his shirt showing through the many holes of the seat of his trousers ... he was a windy word spinner'.

The *Sun* recorded the time that Hughes came to Captains Flat outside Queanbeyan in New South Wales, having been challenged to a debate by the local MP, 'Sully' Sullivan, who was also at the time the state's Minister for Works. Hughes, who had pedalled all the way from Sydney, staying first at Moss Vale, arrived dusty and dishevelled and was called to present his case in 20 minutes. This he did, managing to captivate the tough audience of miners and wipe the floor with a crestfallen Sullivan. After ten minutes for questions the crowd began baying for more entertainment. Watching in the crowd was a young man called Bill Ryrie, who got to his impressive feet and height and offered to provide such by fighting any man in the audience for a stake of £25. When there were no takers to exchange fisticuffs with him (he was known locally as 'The terror of the Mountains') Ryrie entertained the assembly with his impressive whistling skills and 'trilled away like a canary'. Later the 'canary' became Major General Sir Granville de Lane Ryrie KCMG, CB, VD, a Gallipoli hero, and was appointed Australia's High Commissioner in London in 1922.

The budding politician: a game little fellow

The Sydney Domain was fast becoming the city's equivalent of London's Hyde Park Corner and it was here, where earlier he had slept in its caves on first arriving from Brisbane, that Hughes set up his table and began preaching a socialist gospel. In April 1891, the first labour league was formed, largely due to Hughes' advocacy, according to many at the time. He was chosen as a party organiser and toured far and wide arguing both the need for the workers to organise and for support for the nascent Labour Electoral League (later to become the Australian Labor Party): 'We can't have one law for the poor and another for the rich' was a persistent tune in his hymnbook. One account wrote of him touring first on a bike 'until it broke down, then on a horse until it broke down. His shoes wore out, he slept where he could and travelled with the swaggies'. 'We are with you Mr Hughes but the bosses don't like it', said one group of shearers. He visited Currawobity station near Forbes and had tea at the shearers' shed to speak on union matters.

Together with William Holman, who was to become premier of New South Wales, A.G. Yewen, Jim Desmond, Tom Routley, Charlie Pilter and Harry Turnbull he published a socialist tract, 'The New Order', in Pyrmont in 1894. The publication enjoyed considerable resonance among fellow socialists, such as David Storey, Charlie Oakes, George Beeby (later Judge Beeby) and Walter Marks. 'The New Order' called for radical reform and the overthrow of the capitalist system, and Hughes became a regular worshipper at the then temple for Labor free spirits — Leigh House. Other friends included the poet John Farrell, as well as Frank Cotton, George Walker and Louis Lamotte. Another close friend, Frederick William Bumford, known as 'Old Freddy', was vice president of the Waterside Workers Federation.

Also in 1894, ten years after arriving in Australia, Hughes stood at the age of 29 for the New South Wales Parliament in the seat of Lang. Before agreeing to stand he asked for assurances that it was within a one-penny journey from his home in Balmain. The results were: Thyler (Free Trade) 428, Fitzgerald (Protectionist) 273, Butler (Free Trade) 27, Hughes (Labor Electoral League) 533. To celebrate his victory, Hughes was driven around town in a cart by exultant supporters. The Sydney *Daily Telegraph* wrote that he had been in business as a locksmith, and had repaired umbrellas, bicycles and sewing machines. The same day the paper carried stories of striking shearers, of Japan at war with China, and Russian troops on the Korean frontier, and of a man accused of indecency before children, who was sentenced to 72 hours imprisonment and 25 lashes.

Billy Hughes

The Lang constituency would have reminded Hughes very much of the Devil's Acre in London, being equally squalid and disease-ridden, and consisting largely of public houses. When he first entered Parliament there was no payment for members, though later members were awarded £300 a year plus free rail travel anywhere in the state. There was no phone, no typewriters, no cars, radios or aeroplanes. Rooms at the best hotels could be had for 12/6 per night, tailor-made suits cost around two guineas, a bicycle could be had for £2, and food was paid for in pennies rather than pounds. Sydney Harbour was full of tall-masted sailing ships, the population of Australia was three million, and its consolidated revenue £24 million.

Hughes had been active in supporting his friend Holman, who had stood unsuccessfully for Leichhardt (though he won the subsequent election in 1898). Both were instrumental in the early years of the labour movement in winning acceptance by the incipient labour party that loyalty to the decision of caucus was paramount and superseded loyalty to individual views (a position Hughes himself was to abrogate later over the conscription issue). Hughes regarded Holman as a friend through the years, though they were to disagree on a number of issues. Altogether the Labour Electoral League won 36 seats in the aftermath of the Maritime Strike but only Hughes, along with Joseph Cook (Prime Minister 1913–14 and again briefly in 1921) and J.C. Watson (PM for five months in 1904) were trade unionists. On entering the New South Wales Parliament Hughes was described by Keith Murdoch writing in the 'British Australian' as 'a thin delicate nervous little man shabbily garbed, looking hunted, forlorn and miserable'.

The year 1894 also saw Hughes, having accumulated some savings, buying a smallholding at Wilberforce in New South Wales. This was the scene of the infamous ejection of the farmer Bellinger and his family, who had rented the property but, according to Hughes, had failed to deliver on the terms of their agreement. The ejection followed violent confrontation between the two parties with Hughes, attorney-general that he was, suffering a severe blow on the head.

Bellinger took Hughes to court for illegal eviction, won the case and was awarded costs of £255, which Hughes claimed had almost made him bankrupt.

Pursuing syndicalist goals and drumming up support for the new party was an arduous occupation, even for one so blessed with energy and, although there are few records of his activities outside Parliament, the scant records we have from these years give a soupçon of the rigours of his chosen path. The mayor of Burrawong wrote of him and a meeting with the shearers about to participate in the 1894 strike ... 'a game little fellow ... Met Billy Hughes at Big Burrawong Station (where he was a cook). Saw a tired Billy coming on a tired horse. Gave him a meal and saw to his horse. Arranged for a very successful session between him and the shearers the next day.' Many years later a correspondent wrote saying that he had been at the station on that occasion having won the contract to shear 510 000 sheep, the camp consisting of some 800 men who all assembled for roll-call in Hughes' presence.

In 1897, Hughes was on a train, which got stuck in heavy flooding at Bungendore and had to stay there until morning, when it was discovered that after the waters had abated the bridge had been washed away, the engine and carriages were at a perilous angle and the back of the train had been taken by the flood waters. Hughes' few diaries at the NLA are not very revealing but contain some snippets from this period: 'Jan 30 1906 walked to Antarmon 1 mile, from Beara to Car 1 mile, Rowed 3 miles, very hot day. Back to Beara, up hill 1 mile, spoke at conference 6.0, reached home 11.0 Feb 10th Maryborough to Noosa, no breakfast 3rd week, General condition much improved, But not entirely satisfactory. Peaches only, for lunch. Tea 6.30, junket, sour curds, apples nuts raisins. Slept full 8 hours.' Or again 'retired 11.30 Slept well, not tired, ate small piece of chicken, milk junket and apples, drank beer'.

Many years later, people from those early years wrote to him recalling his advocacy of workers' rights: J.J. McGrath from Bathurst, in a letter dated 16 July 1944, wrote 'you initiated me into the Labour movement in an old Stringy Bark Hall at Burraga fifty years ago ... Your proper place is in the ranks of the Labour party.' One Willard Turton wrote on

Billy Hughes

26 July 1944 to say that his father-in-law, Sam Hitchin, one-time proprietor of the *Namoi Independent* in Gunnedah, had been alongside Billy in forming the original Labour Party along with Daly Hall, Tom Roberts, John Cock, Billy Hill and another called Delanders. (Subsequently the preferred spelling was 'Labor'.)

Hughes replied that he too regretted that he was not still in the Labor Party, but would have argued that it was the party which had changed, not him. He did, however, maintain good relations with the labour movement in Britain over the years. He wrote once to Ben Tillett at Transport House in London: 'I long to shake a free leg and let the world see what is to be done to be saved. For I am now as I have always been for the underdog.' Tillett was a Christian socialist, founder of the UK Docker's Union and one of the founders of the British Labour Party and the General Workers Union, who later fully supported British involvement in World War I and had visited Australia. The same day, Hughes wrote to W.A. Appleton, secretary general of the General Federation of Trade Unions in London: 'Ramsay Macdonald always seemed to me to be a black-coated covenanter who had strayed by some unhappy mischance into the Labor camp ... an idealist without anchor ... Sir Stafford Cripps ... He talks like a mechanical doll.'

Hughes' first speech in the New South Wales Parliament included a memorable passage: 'everything is a matter of comparison. To a man who is starving there is wealth in an un-gnawed bone'.[7] A proposal in favour of the opening of shops on Sundays gained momentum, supported by Hughes but without much enthusiasm. Tennis on a Sunday was another matter and he evinced the hope that he would never see such a thing. The biggest issue, however, was the battle for an eight-hour working day, with Henry Parkes chairing the first public meeting in support. It was on this issue that Hughes established himself as a speaker of brilliance with his denunciation of the New South Wales Government. His speech ended '... never in its [the UK Parliament's] wildest acts of madness had it been so asinine as to put on the statute book of that great country a law without any power to enforce it'. A newspaper cutting of the time referred to him walking from Balmain to the Parliament in Macquarie Street, of the calls on him for financial help from his constituents, of donating a pound a week to the Labor Party, of giving away his last shilling to a beggar and relying on a friend for an evening meal.

His attributes of both courage and impetuosity were manifested during the bubonic plague outbreak in Sydney in 1900 when he went from street to street to help the dead and the dying, caring nothing for his own safety, and subsequently being instrumental in provoking the government to intervene with a blistering attack on its inaction. For the *Australian Magazine* he established his reputation in the New South Wales Assembly during the battles over protectionism and free trade with his 'ready tongue, caustic humour and a real knowledge of the problems of working men'. He remained a member until he entered the first federal parliament in 1901 representing West Sydney, which encompassed the Lang electorate. He won the nomination for the federal seat after five exhaustive pre-selection ballots, at which juncture Watson said to him, 'Run for your life, you've been selected'.

Chapter 3

Family strife and political life

*H*ughes' election to the Federal Parliament had meant travelling to Melbourne, where the new Parliament sat, leaving his family in Sydney. It was a time of balancing private and public life.

The first family

The family had moved from Balmain to 6 Merrenburn Avenue near Gore Hill, where the eldest girl, Ethel (born probably in 1892 since she wrote in one letter that she was 14 when her mother died) increasingly had to look after both an ailing mother and her younger siblings — Lily, born at Balmain in 1893; Dolly, born at Annandale in 1895; Ernest, born in Leichhardt in 1897; and Charles, born in Homebush in 1898. The Hughes had lost one son on 9 May 1892 at only 12 months of age, who was buried in Rookwood Cemetery. Arthur, their older step-brother (born in 1885) was also part of the family.

Hughes' wife Elizabeth, née Cutts, died on 1 September 1906 at Osbourne Park, Gore Hill, aged 42, and was buried at the Church of England Cemetery at Gore Hill. She had been seriously ill for some weeks and a sudden attack of paralysis hastened the end of her sufferings. The Reverend Archdeacon Langley conducted the obsequies at home and graveside, and among the mourners was J.C. Watson, the federal Labor leader. The cause of death was given in her death certificate as: 'Heart Failure — Aortic and Mitral Disease. Cerebral embolism.' Her father's profession was described as financier and her mother's maiden name given as Elizabeth McLellan who, according to Farmer Whyte, was descended from Sir Walter Scott. The informant of her death was given as Arthur Hughes, son, of Gore Hill. W.M. Hughes was listed as the husband, and it was stated that she was 20 when she married and that the marriage took place in Melbourne. The reference to Melbourne is odd and cannot pertain to Hughes, since he had never been to the city at this time, arriving in Sydney only in early 1887. What may be the case is that Arthur confused issues, probably deliberately, and was referring to his real father, who had made Elizabeth pregnant in Melbourne where Arthur was born.

It has not been possible to trace any of the children's birth certificates and it may well be that Hughes' apparent failure to register them was deliberate. It is more than probable that Hughes and Elizabeth Cutts never married. No marriage certificate has been located and the eldest daughter, Ethel, battled for years with her father to increase his payments to the girls who had been 'cheated of their birthright'. Diana Williams, Hughes' great-granddaughter, thinks that her grandfather Ernest Williams' view was that, while acknowledging that no marriage certificate had been traced, some form of ceremony had taken place at some stage.

In the NLA records there is a postcard to Hughes from 'Your faithful wife E Hughes' dated 14 August 1906, and a sad little letter sent to him two weeks before she died:

> Dear Will,
>
> Received cheque all right. Sorry you lost the case: hope it will not put you out much: It is very cold here: I feel it dreadfully for you see: my heart troubling me so my blood is thin for indeed I look very blue sometimes; but I trust this will wear away. I hope you are more comfortable with Dear Miss Hennessey: and also that you are keeping in perfect health. The drought is still with us: and eatables seem to get dearer every day ... Bought Ethel a nice piece of music, rather difficult but it won't worry her much: she is so capable ... Good night Will: always remember this: that once I loved you very dearly and though we may drift apart in the future I shall always remain your faithful wife. E Hughes.

These references might support the view that Hughes and Elizabeth had undergone some form of marriage rite, but letters from Ethel make it plain that as regards the law of the land the children were illegitimate and had no legal rights. After Elizabeth's death Hughes spent more and more time in Melbourne while Ethel, apart from visits there to act as Hughes' hostess, stayed in Sydney to look after the younger children until they too went to Melbourne — Dolly and Lily to the Methodist Ladies College and Ernest William ('Bill') and Charles to Melbourne Grammar School. The records of the Methodist College show that both girls entered the college in 1907 and were boarders for the first three terms, and that Lily was 13 in May 1906 and Dolly 11 in March 1906. Their contact address on entry was given as 'William Morris Hughes, National Liberal Club London and Liddiard Street Glenferrie'. Both girls were listed as taking piano as an extra subject. There are no records to indicate when they left the school. The two boys were admitted to the senior school at Melbourne Grammar in 1911, Bill thereafter going to Richmond Agricultural College in New South Wales. Charles is recorded as later marrying Margaret Stewart, daughter of R.W. Short.

Crossing swords

On the political front, Hughes was as involved as ever. Though he had always been a supporter of the move towards Federation, Hughes had voted against the constitution drawn up by the 1897 convention largely because he felt that as then drafted it would benefit the conservative elements in politics. He favoured equal voting rights for men and women, a lower and an upper house with sole powers for initiating legislation, and amendment of money bills vested in the lower house. In the event, a largely conservative constitution was adopted for the new Federation, far removed from the original republican proposals advocated by John Dunmore Lang in the 1850s and later by the Sydney *Bulletin*.

If two overriding sentiments or beliefs remained ever bright with Hughes, they were his abiding sense of Australia's identity in the world, albeit as part of the British Empire, and a persistent belief in the notion of 'civitas' or civic responsibility. Later, in the Fisher Government, Hughes was to become the main proponent for extending federal powers, the control of large corporations and the nationalisation of monopolies, proposals that were lost in the referendum of 1911 with the supporters of state rights prevailing, among whom was his old friend Holman. It was not surprising that Holman was a fervent supporter of state rights, coming as he did from the largest and most prosperous state in the country. (Even at 79, Hughes backed another bid to extend federal power, at variance with the majority of his own supporters.) Holman described him as the Labor Party's outstanding exponent of the federation principle. If Alfred Deakin, three times PM in the period 1903–1910, was the father of Federation, Hughes was, through the years, its most steadfast exponent. Of the other fathers of Federation, Hughes wrote: 'Sir Henry Parkes — a great man, a great democrat'; Edmund Barton, Australia's first Prime Minister (1901–03) 'the noblest Roman of them all'; George Reid, PM for 11 months in 1904–05 (and leader of the conservative free traders who later fused with Deakin's liberals), 'wonderful man, master of repartee, never at a loss'; and Deakin, 'orator'.

He and Deakin crossed swords often in the House, with the honours more or less even — Deakin more superficially genteel but not the less effective. On one occasion, responding to an attack by Hughes on his record, Deakin expostulated, 'I deny it, I deny it, I deny it'; Hughes remained silent until the Speaker enquired whether he had finished, to which Hughes replied, 'No Mr Speaker, I'm waiting for the cock to crow'. After one acerbic outburst by Hughes in a speech at Ballarat, Deakin described him as: 'The ill bred urchin whom one sees dragged from a tart shop kicking and screaming as he goes.' Subsequently Deakin regretted his words and made a handsome apology in Parliament. (Deakin too, had a Welsh background, his mother Sarah having been born and brought up in Llanarth, a village near Abergavenny in South Wales. Although there is no evidence that this Welsh background meant much to Deakin, his house in South Yarra in Melbourne where he died in 1919 was called Llanarth.)

The rough and tumble of the political game was balm to Hughes' soul but there was a very clear distinction between his fierce demeanour and performance in political debate and his comparative generosity to political opponents outside the political cockpit. Invariably his remarks on the death of political adversaries were warm and unsullied by the trauma of past enmity. He was instrumental in obtaining a barony for a certain Mr Forrest, a member of Parliament who once referred to him as 'one of those little black things you find under big flat stones' (though Hughes perhaps did so largely to remove a nuisance from the game). He was helpful to Frank Anstey's wife when her husband was ailing. When Chifley fell ill in 1950 Hughes wrote to him: 'Forget about the rushing, foaming cataract of world events — about politics, about everything. I've been through the mill. I know. What's the world to a man when his wife is a widow?' He found it hard to comprehend personal attacks on him outside the chambers of parliamentary debate; of the many prime ministers he had known, Hughes, late in life remarked: 'I've known them all and worked with or against them all — like the curate's egg they were good in parts.'

As a parliamentary performer he had few equals, and had the capacity to put an opponent down with a minimum of words and 'the epigrammatic force of his comments', but his particular forte was perhaps in being able to hold and often sway a hostile audience, exhibiting considerable courage as evinced years earlier with the wharfies. When one very antipathetic audience drowned his speech as soon as he had uttered the first word, 'Gentlemen', in a lull he carried on with cocky defiance: 'Alright I'll withdraw that remark'. Instead of lynching him the crowd guffawed with laughter, which says perhaps as much for the crowd as it does for him. In one parliamentary debate Hughes went on the attack: 'The honourable member is not fit to swill milk with pigs'. When the member objected Hughes said: 'Very well the honourable member is fit to swill milk with pigs'.

'Matchless courage'

The first Labor administration came to power in 1904 and J. C. Watson, the new Prime Minister, invited Hughes to be a member of his cabinet. The Melbourne *Punch* of 23 June 1904 described the rising star as: 'a man of middle height of frail build with very long legs and a habit of stuffing his hands into his trouser pockets — he had very long arms... Mr Hughes is noted for saneness and common sense.' Another wrote: 'Mr Hughes despite his radicalism is fundamentally a British Imperialist', and another: 'Billy Hughes, Australia's youngest old man. Impatient with humbug, he has a knack of getting to the centre of a problem.' Offered the attorney-general portfolio, Hughes declined on the basis that he did not have the necessary legal experience for the job, but did accept the post of Minister for External Affairs. It was only in the previous year that he had completed his legal studies, being called to the New South Wales Bar on 19 November 1903. Later he felt qualified to accept the attorney-generalship when Fisher became Prime Minister in 1908, and took silk in 1909, becoming a king's counsel.

H.V. Evatt, one of Australia's long-serving Ministers of Foreign Affairs and, like Hughes, also to split the Labor Party, was to wonder, in his book on Holman,[1] at Hughes' diligence, hard work and application in qualifying for the Bar given his other commitments — the trade union movement, parliamentary duties and a family. Evatt believed that this involved even greater difficulty than faced by Holman, who had also qualified as a lawyer, as well as 'matchless courage'. According to Evatt, Hughes and Holman in their early labour movement days had no strong views whether to stand for the federal or state parliaments and resolved the matter by tossing a coin, with Hughes winning the federal option. For Evatt, Hughes 'was not a reactionary, quite the contrary'. His legal activities were largely concerned with trade union causes and defence of individual trade unionists, especially on arbitration issues, for which he became much sought after. Having been a leading force behind the setting up of the Waterside Workers Federation, his negotiating skills were again in evidence in a nasty coal strike in 1909 when his intervention prevented it escalating into a general strike.

He exhibited the same ability to defuse potentially damaging industrial relations strife in 1916, again involving coalminers, but this time aided by the fact that the then miners' leader, a man called Willis, was Welsh. With a strike being threatened, Hughes told Willis, 'Don't go on strike, I'll fix it', which he did. He never regarded the law as his future career; rather it was a tool to aid his political progress, but nevertheless his respect for the profession was great and the honorary law degree he received towards the end of his life brought much satisfaction. When he died he was still an honorary Master of the Grays Inn Bench in London.

As regards his performance in the Federal Parliament, *Punch* wrote in 1908: 'He has not a striking personality, he is surrounded by an air of insignificance. He is short and squat and narrow-chested, with bowed legs, wide cruel-lipped mouth, ears which evoke derision, and a knotted, gnarled face ... but he is far and away the most successful and cleverest ... to have led the Labour Party ... and serve the cause of the worker.' (He was in fact not the leader, only the deputy leader from 1907 to 1915.)

The first Australian federal government under Prime Minister Barton stood for protectionism and a White Australia Policy, and one of its first acts was to pass the *Immigration Restriction Act*, which banned all non-Europeans from settling in the country. In 1906–07 some 4000 Kanakas (Pacific Islanders) were sent home as a consequence of the policy, including families who had lived in Australia for two generations and had been brought in from the Pacific Islands largely to work the cane fields in Queensland because it was believed at the time that white folks could not manage the heat. Deakin wrote with an abundance of honesty in this regard: 'It is not the bad qualities of these alien races that make them so dangerous to us, it is their inexhaustible energy, their power of applying themselves to new tasks, their endurance and low standard of living that make them such competitors.' Hughes and the Labor Party were of the same mind: 'Australia was a predominantly British country after all', but he would have little truck with protectionism: free trade was his credo and 'The Wealth of Nations' his gospel. He was to enunciate on the White Australia Policy on many occasions during his career: 'It was a policy upon which all parties were agreed, a national policy of defence not defiance.' Hughes' views in this regard reflected the convictions of the majority of people at the time. He claimed to have been one of those responsible for its introduction and 'always regarded it as vital to the present and future welfare of Australia'. However, he also on one occasion admitted that the policy had no moral basis.

In reality, the policy had its origins back in 1848 with the great influx of Chinese into Australia provoking riots in the goldfields, and in New South Wales some 13 years later, with legislation introduced in 1861 to regulate Chinese immigration. On another occasion Hughes wrote: 'The attitude of Australia towards Eastern peoples is not one of arrogant assertion of superiority over other races but is dictated by the instinct of self-preservation ... They [Australians] do not regard Asiatics as inferior but as different from themselves.' And on 30 September 1944:

> The White Australia Policy is not like Nazism — a glorification of race or colour — we do not by that policy proclaim the superiority of the White race — as we do not discriminate against Coloured peoples because of their colours but because of their low living standards. If our gates were left wide open the coloured race of Asia would pour in and offer to sell their labour for far less than that which Australian workers have won.

Although the White Australia Policy was overturned in 1964, Hughes' views were to find temporary support in the appeal of Pauline Hanson and her followers over 50 years later.

Chapter 4

'Billy Bach' — the little Welshman

Among interested researchers in Wales an open question has always been: did he speak the Welsh language, and if so to what extent? Llansantffraid today has hardly any Welsh speakers and we do not know how much Welsh was spoken by his aunt in the house in Llandudno or at Winllan Farm; nor is there any evidence that Welsh was spoken at the Hughes home in London or that his mother was Welsh speaking, although his father did 'speak the language of heaven'. In Hughes' handwritten draft of an altercation with Lloyd George he included the Welsh he maintained he had used: 'Ah cae soon, caer I Diawl' ('Ah shut up. Go to the Devil'). The written Welsh is poor, but spoken it would have been understood by Lloyd George. It suggests that Hughes had never studied Welsh, and relied on the language he acquired at school in Llandudno and on the farm in Llansantffraid.

A letter in the archives of the National Library of Wales records the author's opinion that Hughes did speak some Welsh and that he was a good speaker 'but lacked Lloyd George's style, craft and farsightedness'. Hughes spoke regularly at functions on March the First (organised to commemorate Wales National Day and Wales' Patron Saint David) especially in Sydney but also in Newcastle, Melbourne and elsewhere. A number of these speeches, in typed and note form, are to be found in his papers. They are orotund and declamatory, as was the style of the day, and invariably claim the Welsh as the original

Britons: 'Wales was Wales before England was England ... at least 2000 years before the Saxons.'[1] He liked to think of Wales as 'the oldest brother'. Elsewhere he talked about the Welsh 'girding the Earth'. He often took pride in the accomplishments of people of Welsh origin: 'In Sydney the Hughes are stars of the first magnitude. Leaving myself out there is J. Hughes the Taxation Commissioner and F.W. Hughes, a man as rich as Croesus.' During an address in Melbourne, Hughes was reported as having said that it was intolerable that the people of Australia were allowed to grow up in ignorance of Welsh — the 'finest language in the World'.

Hughes was clearly regarded by his contemporaries as a Welshman, a perception that prevailed throughout his long life. The *Herald and Weekly Times* of Melbourne drew his attention on one occasion to the fact that the first Prince of Wales was born on 25 April (in 1284), a date that later became ANZAC Day, adding 'As a good Welshman this might be of interest to you'. He was asked to become a patron of the Welsh National Eisteddfod in Caernarfon in 1923. A frequent correspondent was Charles Lloyd Jones, managing director of David Jones, which was to become and still is one of the largest chain of department stores in Australia, and grandson of the founder, a Welsh-speaking Welshman who hailed from Llandeilo in South Wales. The original David Jones opened his first store in Melbourne on 24 May 1838, sold out to a syndicate in 1857 and returned to Wales, only to come back to Australia three years later and open a new store. Writing to Hughes on 3 February 1926 Charles begged him, 'as a son of Gwalia ... to be Chairman of a meeting to plan for St David's Day and amalgamate the various Sydney Welsh Societies'.

At the time there were three Welsh societies in the city and typical of Welsh expatriates the world over they found it immensely difficult ever to coalesce into one group. According to one commentator, the history of the various Welsh movements in Sydney had in the main been a series of 'spasmodic bursts'. This amoebic tendency is almost a national characteristic, referred to in Wales as an example of 'cythraul y canu' ('the devil of singing') — a phenomenon with its origins in the great

Welsh tradition of hymn singing (which had its heyday perhaps during the Depression) and saw choirs and indeed churches divide and split over minor disagreements resulting in completely disproportionate feelings of bitterness and angst. In Sydney today there are still three Welsh societies, and memories of past slights or disagreements real or imagined still hold sway among some of their members.

Charles Lloyd Jones wrote frequently as president of the Welsh Society requesting Hughes' presence, participation or speech, sending on one occasion many 'Welsh and Australian thank yous for your kindness. Why you should shower these kindnesses on a poor but honest draper is beyond my comprehension ...' Hughes and Jones remained such friends through the years that when Hughes sent clothes to the store for dry-cleaning they were personally addressed to Sir Charles Lloyd Jones. In 1938, the store held a big commemoration of 100 years in Australia, with Hughes and Lady Mary in attendance as honoured guests and with a dinner menu showing a girl dressed in Welsh traditional costume.

Nearly all of Hughes' references to Wales and the Welsh language are to be found in the speeches he gave to Welsh audiences in Australia and Britain or in letters to Welsh correspondents. This is not surprising perhaps, but one would have expected to see occasional rhetorical flourishes concerning his Celtic patrimony and cultural inheritance glistening in his addresses to other audiences or in his political speeches; however, there are but few. He sometimes inserted the odd Welsh phrase or salutation in replies to letters or notes — invariably mis-spelt. In this regard, his approach was consistent with his tendency or character trait to compartmentalise: the whole matter of his Welsh background was pigeonholed, to be brought out like a Sunday suit, dusted down and paraded on special occasions only.

Once the ABC sent him a letter inviting him to broadcast a goodwill message in English and Welsh, and followed up with a suggested form of words for him to use. He wrote a note to his secretary: 'I shall have to let this go ... illness, pressing public engagements etc'. Usually he accepted any offers of broadcasting and one suspects that on this occasion the refusal had more to do with his inability to do it in Welsh than any other. The BBC also asked him to do a jubilee broadcast in Welsh, to which he replied, 'certainly you know nothing about the Welsh language or you would not have asked me to make a speech in it'.

Yet just when one has come to the conclusion that, as far as knowledge of the Welsh language was concerned, his was perfunctory, one comes across a letter half in Welsh, half in English from a Miss Enid Beary Torrington of North Devon who clearly had at one time been very close to Hughes but of whom this is the only trace in his papers. She begins: 'Fy annwyl a charedig ffrind. Daeth y blwch ryfeddol yn ddiogel i'm llaw ac nis gallaf cael geiriau yn ddigon cymmwys …' ('My Dear and generous friend. The amazing package arrived safely and I cannot find the right words to thank you properly …') The Welsh in the letter is of a high standard, despite some orthographic glitches, and one has to presume that the writer would have known that Hughes' understanding of the language was sufficient to appreciate this paean of thanks, with England then in the grips of hard times, ration books and tightened belts.

Indeed there were frequent requests to him for food parcels and equally frequently he obliged, even to complete strangers who wrote to him, 'The most respected Welshman and kind Sir …' Many wrote following his two trips to Wales in 1916 and 1932. A Mr Oldfield informed him that he was head teacher at the Church of England school when Hughes had visited during World War I and donated a stained-glass window in memory of his mother. Hughes had also given the school a photograph, which, now some 30 years later, had regrettably disappeared. 'Would it be at all possible for Hughes to supply a new photo please?' asked Mr Oldfield.

Three months before Hughes' death, a Welsh lady named Ivie Price, who obviously had known him well and for many years, wrote: 'Diolch am eich llythyr a wnaeth imi chwerthin am wythnos. Tybed pa "vitamins" a gymerwch i gadw eich hiwmor mor llym.' ('Thank you for your letter which made me laugh for a week. I wonder what "vitamins" you are taking to keep your wit so keen'.) Ivie was also a regular sender of birthday cards and Christmas greetings, often in Welsh.

He was in frequent receipt of missives and requests from an array of churches and, perhaps surprisingly, maintained more than tolerable relations with all. The Welsh Presbyterian Church in Sydney wrote on one occasion enclosing an 'englyn' — a Welsh poetic form which in its condensed brevity has been compared with the Japanese haiku:

> Anian rydd i'm haelioni-yng nghanol
> Angenion mae'n gweini
> At aelwydydd tlodi
> Llifa'r aur o'i llaw fawr hi.

> (May I be granted generosity, which acts in the midst of need, to ensure a flow of riches from its great hand to poor homes.)

Letters from abroad

Correspondents who wrote to Hughes from many parts of the world referred naturally to him as a Welshman. One such was Leo Amery, whom he first met in 1907 at the Maritime Conference and who clearly held him in considerable regard. Amery, an MP from 1911 to 1945, had been political secretary to the war cabinet from 1916 to 1918 and to the Paris Peace Conference. Subsequently, he led the Conservative coup which toppled Lloyd George in 1922 and later was appointed first lord of the admiralty and then British colonial secretary. He had warmed to Hughes for his robust and pragmatic approach to the conduct of both the war and the peace negotiations, finding the theorising of US president Woodrow Wilson abstract, distasteful and non-productive. The respect and liking was mutual: Hughes was particularly grateful for Amery's role as prime mover in getting agreement that the Dominion premiers become members of the war cabinet and deliberate as equals on the conduct of the war. A letter of 4 February 1946 from Amery mentioned Wales:

> My dear Hughes
> I have just been addressing a great Europe Day meeting in Cardiff. Naturally I led off by buttering up gallant little Wales referring to the red-haired Welsh woman whom we claimed as our great Queen

Elizabeth and the only dictator to whom England had ever submitted, the Welshman who would have been called Williams if his father had not pasted the more Saxon label of Cromwell over the Williams ... two Welshmen who had done most for the Empire ... the one buried in the land of his fathers and the other still alive and very much kicking in the little continent which he had adopted.

In December 1921, Amery had written regarding Ireland's likely designation as a dominion: 'It only remains for the same to be done to England and Scotland leaving Wales to bear the main burden of sustaining the Imperial fabric. In that case you had better come home and see your native land through its difficulties.' And when Hughes was selected to stand again for federal parliament at the age of 87, Amery telegraphed: 'Delighted Australia still keeps her Billy on the boil'. A further telegram congratulated him on his 50 years in Parliament: 'I dips me lid'. A month before his death, Amery wrote remembering the time he personally had spent trying to maintain harmony between Hughes and Lloyd George during the Peace Conference. His efforts had presumably been successful since 'music and Welsh hymns' had followed.

Another who regularly sent greetings or encouragement was author Richard Hughes. These were usually in the form of telegrams, addressed 'to the Head of the Australian Hughes clan' and apologising that the Japanese post office would not accept greetings in the Welsh language, such as on the occasion when Hughes surpassed Lloyd George's record as a parliamentarian in April 1949. Among Billy Hughes' papers was a book, *Gem Selections — Songs of Wales*, given to him in 1921, and copies of *The Welsh Australian* (one such, dated Saturday 19 June 1937, recorded Tommy Farr's retention of the Empire Heavyweight Boxing Title, and elsewhere advertised a single and double room for rent at 8 shillings and 14 shillings respectively — per week!). He also kept a book entitled *Montgomery Worthies* by R. Williams, headed 'Ym mhob gwlad y megir glew' ('Brave men are born in every country').

So what are we to make of these scattered clues? Typical of the man, the evidence of his degree of Welshness is inconclusive and the verdict on his knowledge of the Welsh language uncertain. One thing is reasonably clear: he always took pride in his Welsh background, and there is not the slightest indication that he ever denied that background or found anything but delight in it. There are some suggestions that he did not parade his origins in his early years in Australia: none of his six children from Elizabeth Cutts were given Welsh names, for example, nor is there any evidence that they were made aware of their Welsh heritage or had any knowledge of Welsh history, culture or language. And yet the daughter of his marriage to Mary Campbell was given a quintessential Welsh girl's name: Myfanwy.

Hughes and Lloyd George

Hughes' trip to Britain saw his first meeting with one of the silken-voiced orators of the day, fellow Welshman David Lloyd George, who chaired the London Conference in his capacity as president of the Board of Trade in the Asquith administration. Later, Lloyd George was to write that Hughes, 'put his views with all the tenacity of the ancient race to which you and I belong and which has enabled us to survive 2000 years of persecution'. (Hughes was to expatiate on the same theme in an after-dinner speech, on the theme 'Wales and the War', to the Cymmrodorion Society at the Trocadero in London during his next visit to the United Kingdom in 1916: 'I feel I am in the presence of my kinsmen ... The day of the Celt. For a thousand years they [the English] have persecuted us who have now called the Celt to lead their respective nations in their hour of need.'[2])

The visit to the UK in 1907 also saw him begin a career in journalism, writing a weekly column for the *Daily Telegraph* from October 1907 to October 1911. Hughes and Lloyd George were obviously attracted to each other and carried on an intermittent correspondence over the years. On one occasion, Hughes recalled the

Maritime Conference and walking with a *Daily Mail* reporter who referred to Lloyd George as a 'little struggling Welsh solicitor'. Hughes continued:

> ... the reporter being evidently of the opinion that I was an Australian duly appreciative of the abysmal gap between the English and these inferior Celts. When I told him that I was, as he could see, little, that I was Welsh, and that although not a solicitor I was a barrister, he looked a little upset. Dash it all, when it came to a showdown, when the Empire was blowing like a harpooned whale, who saved it? Who ran it? — not the English — but this little Welsh solicitor.

Nevertheless, there seems always to have been an arm's length distance between them: invariably they addressed each other by their surnames, an affectation today perhaps, but then a custom of the times. And, despite a degree of warmth and shared drama over the years of World War I, Hughes, as in many of his relations with colleagues throughout his life, retained a hardness, exhibiting what others noted as his want of the 'softer emotions'. Three days after opening the local ninth Annual Drummoyne Eisteddfod in 1923, he drafted a note regarding a proposed visit by Lloyd George to Australia which, notwithstanding the relations between them, advised that Lloyd George be told clearly that the government would not be able to pay his expenses, out and back. This too could have been due to Hughes' tightfistedness in all money matters. In Wales he would have been known as a 'Cardi', someone who hailed from Cardiganshire in Wales where the population was renowned for having excessively deep pockets and very short arms. Being 'careful with one's money' was the usual euphemism for such people — a characteristic often found in people of both sexes who had become financially secure, even rich, but had sprung from an impoverished background.

A favourite story of Hughes about Lloyd George, which he used on many occasions, was of an attack on him at a public meeting in Caernarfon in North Wales by the then Bishop of St Asaph for supporting the disestablishment of the Church of Wales. Wales was almost one hundred per cent non-conformist, but people were obliged by law to pay tithes for the upkeep of what they regarded as Anglican, not Welsh, churches. Later the same day Lloyd George was called to reply. A man called Brawd, the foreman of the slate quarries, said by way of introduction: 'A little time ago the Bishop of St Asaph was speaking in this hall and the biggest liar I ever heard in my life he was but', and he turned to Lloyd George, 'thank God we have a match for him here tonight in Lloyd George.'

On 8 August 1921, Hughes unveiled a statue of Lloyd George, which stands in the main square in Caernarfon with its magnificent castle as a backdrop (where the English King Edward I reportedly announced from the ramparts that his firstborn son was to be named the Prince of Wales). On another occasion Lloyd George commented, 'I see my friend Bill is in another Government — clever man — Bill — lots of courage' and in 1937 wrote to 'My dear Hughes' asking for a photograph of Hughes to insert into his Peace book. In Lloyd George's war memoirs Hughes is described as a 'pugnacious little Welshman, acute mind, phenomenal energy', adding 'He and Asquith did not get on too well. They would not.' Included too is the famous Low cartoon showing a raging Billy at the Cabinet table and Asquith beseeching Lloyd George to speak to him in Welsh to pacify him. Of Lloyd George, Hughes once remarked, 'You might think I'm a bit of an autocrat. Perhaps I am. Perhaps I have to be, but compared to Lloyd George, I'm a proper dove.'

In a letter of 4 October 1945, Hughes wrote to a lady who taught Welsh in Sydney: 'I recall vividly a meeting at Conway where Lloyd George spoke in Welsh and being called upon to follow him I asked — in Welsh — why don't you speak in English — which shows you to what extent English has overlain our native tongue. Your Welsh class is a novel feature in these degenerate days.' After Lloyd George's death, his widow, Lady Frances Lloyd, asked Hughes to lend his name in support of the Lloyd George Memorial Appeal (to build a memorial college in the village of his boyhood), to which he obliged and sent a donation.

Billy Hughes

Some commentators have suggested that Hughes was a kind of March the First Welshman who wore his Welshness on his sleeve rather than in his heart, that it was a useful prop to underline his own specificity or uniqueness and distinguish himself from the hoi polloi of English and Irish extraction. If this was the case, he was exceptionally consistent in the pretence, for throughout his career he never claimed to be other than of Welsh origin, took obvious pride in extolling the virtues of the Celtic race, regularly accepted invitations to speak at Welsh functions and without fail answered scores of letters from Wales and Welsh people. Frequently he included some Welsh aphorism or greeting in his letters and named his house at Sassafras 'Ty Coed' ('Wood House'). Replying to a specific enquiry whether he was Welsh, he wrote, 'I am Welsh but like Lloyd George I was not born in Wales but in London'. Evatt, in his speech in Parliament on Hughes' death, said 'Mr Hughes was a Welshman … but his supreme devotion was to Australia'. Welsh speakers during and after his rise to international fame referred to him in their language as Billy Bach ('Little Willy') — affectionate but not without a touch of cheekiness, very proud that one of their countrymen had become Prime Minister in a distant land.

On his return to Australia Hughes began a part-time career in journalism, and it was in *Life* magazine of 15 September 1907 that he commented acerbically but with acuity that, 'The Government of England … remains the special perquisite of a class … the English are always a little suspicious of a brilliant man … the keystone to success in England and Greater Britain is excellence in public speaking'.

Chapter 5

The slippery slope

On return to Australia in 1907, Hughes was quickly immersed in both the active pursuit of politics, but even more in serious contemplation and analysis of which paths the young Commonwealth should be treading. In a series of articles for the Sydney *Daily Telegraph*, written between 1907 and 1911 under the general title of 'The Case for Labor', he surveyed the beginnings and development of the Australian Labor Party, formed from the heterogeneous elements of the old Solidarity Party. The articles are as reasoned a treatise as any of Hughes' subsequent offerings, and go a long way to offsetting the arguments that he was largely a windbag who, in sparrow fashion, lived on the scattered crumbs of abler men. In these articles he examined the costs of unrestrained competition, analysed the rapacity of private enterprise and demanded a fair wage for all, and did so with a marked degree of intellectual acumen, original thinking and fine writing.

Within the ALP Hughes' brilliance was recognised but there were disparate elements not prepared to give him the reins of power, preferring the Scotsman Andrew Fisher as leader. Among Labor's ranks there were some who held great reservations concerning the young so-called intellectuals like Hughes rising to eminence in the party. Other more conservative cadres worried about Hughes' militancy and links with the union movement. In his election appeal in West Sydney for the 1910 federal election, Hughes outlined what he regarded as his contribution in both state and federal parliaments:

- principal role in having the Early Closing Act put on the statute book of New South Wales;
- his defence of the White Australia Policy;

- a similar role in getting the City Franchise Act passed, which destroyed plural voting for the election of the City Council;
- compulsory arbitration;
- old age pensions;
- his fight for an effective Defence Policy, unceasing advocacy of Compulsory Military Training from 1901 onwards; and
- his support for the construction of the Trans-continental Railway and development of the Northern Territory.

Labor won a large majority and Hughes was appointed attorney-general, a post he held at different times for longer than any subsequent Australian politician. More importantly, he became PM Fisher's right-hand man and increasingly ran the ship of state — 'with his pen', as he once boasted. This was recognised in the press: 'for years it was to be a case not exactly of the captain wearing the uniform and the first mate running the ship — there was quality to Fisher — but at least of the first mate's judgement being what mattered most in the monsoon season.'[1] For *Punch*, Fisher was Prime Minister only in name.

Mary

On 26 June 1911, Hughes married a nurse, Mary Campbell. Mary was born 6 June 1874 at Burrandong, Macquarie River, in New South Wales, the second daughter of Thomas and Mary Ann Campbell (née Burton), who owned a large flour mill. It is possible that this was the same station he had visited at some time in the 1900s on the tramp for the party, that he and Mary met on that occasion and that a spark of romance had been ignited between them. The marriage took place at Christ Church, South Yarra, and there are brief references to the wedding in the *Argus* and *Age* of that month. The papers reported that Ethel, Hughes' eldest daughter, was present at the wedding and had recently been married herself, that the wedding was a quiet one — his colleagues were unaware of the event, although later the newlyweds were given a wedding present of a plated tea-set by the Australian Parliament. The *Age* added that the bride was of a rather studious turn of mind and had literary leanings.

The slippery slope

Instead of a honeymoon, bride, groom and Ethel went motoring, with Hughes, as was his wont, driving at high speed, resulting in an accident on a bumpy road and, for him, a broken rib. After the marriage, various accounts suggest that he progressively cut himself off from his older associations and even from his first family. However, the evidence is mixed; certainly, having moved from Sydney to Melbourne, he would already have been distanced from his comrades in the Sydney labour and trade union movements, and travel in those years was arduous and time consuming (the journey from Sydney to Melbourne taking a full day). His correspondence, however, shows that he remained in regular contact with his children, sometimes spasmodically, and with some more frequently than others.

According to some members of the family, Mary was not over-endowed with intelligence and regarded the first family as an embarrassment and a cut or two below her in terms of social class. However, all reports suggest that she had nevertheless a calming and emollient influence on Hughes throughout their life together, accompanying him on most of his travels. With her nursing background she was able to look after him during his numerous bouts of sickness, and help with his more chronic conditions. For people who knew her, she exhibited a stoic acceptance of the trials which being married to one such as Hughes implied. *Punch* was to write: 'Dame Mary Hughes [she had been honoured in 1922 for services rendered during the war], who in the days when her husband was king, gave the impression that she was scared to open her mouth for fear that Billy would put his foot in it.' And while again there are no written records to even intimate what Hughes' feelings were towards her, some elements in her letters to him suggest a depth of feeling and regard which was genuine, and her letters contain touches of unintended humour: 'I do love you, nobody could love you more'; 'my most beloved of husbands'; 'My dear Will, I am indeed very sorry I spoke to you as I did this morning and I hope never to do so again. You are very kind to me and I love you very much. My feet are so terrible that the pain of them goes to my head and besides the dog was snoring the whole night.'

Diane Langmore paints a picture of a well-meaning but intellectually limited lady made occasional fun of by a father and daughter who shared a much closer bond of empathy between themselves than existed between either and her. Writing to a friend by the surname of Gullett, who had been a journalist in Paris covering the Peace Conference, Hughes once commented of Mary, 'the poor dear rambles a good deal; but she means well', and on another occasion, 'I've known my wife a good many years but this is the first time I've heard her laugh at a joke at the right time'. Their only daughter, Helen Beatrice Myfanwy, was born 9 August 1915; Mary would have liked to have had more children but was unable to following a hysterectomy.

Three years after Hughes' death, Mary was asked by a reporter to indicate what were the things she remembered most warmly about her late husband. She replied: how he stood up to Wilson at the Peace Conference; how he refused to sell their house in Melbourne, although they needed the money, because it would have meant ejecting an old couple who had been their caretakers for years; how he insisted they always had a supply of blankets to give to old diggers who frequently came to their door for help during the Depression; and how he would regularly read the Bible to her and her niece.

In December 1912, Hughes leased a house, 'Merriman', at Barbers Road, Auburn, but by April the next year the family had moved to a house at 35 Herbert Street, St Kilda, called 'Woolundunga', for a rent of £3 per week. At one stage they also lived in Malvern on the corner of McInley and Claremount Avenues, where Hughes had to build on an additional room to house a billiard table he had bought. They also lived in Cotham Road, Kew, which Hughes leased from 1913 to 1923 and which Charles his youngest son gave as his address when he volunteered for service in the war. The house was in the art nouveau style with wide verandas and coloured glass windows. At the rear were stables where Hughes kept his horse, allowing it to roam the nearby streets despite the objections of the Kew Council.

The slippery slope

Money matters

An intriguing letter came to him on 2 June 1913 from one F.S. Whaley of the Warrigal Club congratulating him on his re-election and adding: 'However we may differ in politics you know that I have no sympathy with the publication (only intended to injure you politically) of details of your private business and of any interest your wife may have had in Bellambi shares.' Hughes had been attacked in the press for hypocrisy for being an important shareholder in the company when he and the government were conducting a campaign against trusts. Apologies to Hughes were subsequently printed when it was acknowledged that he had only ever had but a few shares in Bellambi and had sold them at least a year earlier. Two years later the Melbourne *Sunday Age* carried a story that Hughes had received a sum of £500 from the founder of Aspro, George Nicholas, for having awarded him an exclusive licence to manufacture in Australia when Hughes was attorney-general. Allegedly, Hughes' friend Frank Austen had been given £500 as well. According to Nicholas's widow, it was Hughes who had ensured that Nicholas was awarded this money for being the first to come up with a replacement for Bayer aspirin.

Mary always had problems in getting money out of Hughes. According to family friends, Hughes always 'kept Mary short', and there are several instances of her writing to remind him that she had not received her monthly allowance: 'Will you please send me my February cheque'. Referring to 'Elderslie', the house they bought in Lindfield, Sydney, she said it 'is a very difficult house to run, I wish we could sell it'. Or again, a very terse note: 'Dear Will, Will you please let me have my allowance of £25 pounds from June up to December, Mary.' She once complained to a friend, Agnes, that she didn't have enough money to have her hair set. Much embarrassment was caused locally, with outstanding bills to local shopkeepers in the Lindfield area such a problem that Mary was refused credit. One skeleton in the family cupboard was that she was believed to be somewhat light-fingered, so that before going to stay with friends Hughes would make sure that any attractive pieces of silverware were kept well out of sight, or rather touch. Even domestically it appears that he felt he had to exercise a marked degree of control in regard to her predilections. A diary entry for 1938 in shorthand noted, 'Whiskey in bookcase; Key in wallet-office; Scent in cupboard-office'.

This prudence on his part extended to Mary's shopping as well, which may partly explain why he exercised so much oversight on her expenditure. A letter of 8 September 1919 marked 'confidential' conveys information from a Melbourne law firm, Blake and Riggall, sent to various firms: 'The Hon WM Hughes requests us to ask you to note that as Mrs Hughes has an allowance all her transactions with you should be on a cash basis.' A subsequent note came from the Commercial Bank concerning returned cheques of Mrs Hughes. Eleven years later there was a note to him from David Jones saying that, as per his request, in future no goods would be supplied to Dame Mary without his personal authority. One letter was sent to her from David Jones charging her account, since they could not charge anything to her husband's account without his written order. In her diaries Mary regularly recorded the extent of her overdraft. Fadden wrote of Hughes saying of Mary: 'She doesn't know what a budget is … but brother try to charge her fifteen pence for a shilling cabbage and see how you get on', and of Fadden wrestling with the national budget: 'Brother, you worry too much. Damn the budget. Angels can't do more than their best. After all you can dress a harlot to look like an innocent bride.'

The allowance made to his wife varied a little, but the regular monthly amounts could not fairly be described as ungenerous. In the latter six months of 1939 she received:

26 July, £27

26 August, £27.13.6

5 October, £28

18 October, £28.3

15 November, £30

19 December, £29.12

Hughes had had only 2/6 when he landed in Brisbane in 1884. By dint of continuous hard work in his early Australian years, as well as application and shrewd investments, he had become comfortably well off and by 1930 was in receipt of an annual income of £4112 (worth around $290 000 in today's money). Of this, £1000 represented his parliamentary salary, the additional income coming from:

Director's fees, £300

Profit on book, £250

Interest on Commonwealth loan, £1707

Taxable dividends, £855.

One element of his director's fees came from the Amalgamated Wireless Company of Australia. The company had been formed as early as 1913, but in 1922 the government acquired a controlling interest in it and appointed some ministers to the board — a practice unthinkable today. Hughes was one of those nominated and remained a director until he died. His federal tax bill in 1938/39 was £610.9.11. By 1944, this had risen only to a figure of £745, and in 1947 to £1194. Medical bills were consistently high, running at around £520 per year.

Power, the great aphrodisiac

Hughes, for the most part, was very cautious in his relations with the opposite sex. He would rarely get into a controversy with women and would evade argument with a joke, believing that women were seldom susceptible to reason and had to be manoeuvred around. According to Mary's niece Viti Snodgrass, Hughes had fought shy of marrying, having once said to her that 'marriage was a lottery and you don't want to be in too great a hurry to take a ticket'. However, having fathered seven children, six of them in the space of 10 years, there can be few doubts that Hughes had a healthy libido. And while there are few definitive indications of liaisons after his marriage to Mary, there are hints in the correspondence which suggest that a romantic heart beat within that carapace of knobbly and pachydermatous politician.

All would have agreed that Hughes was very far from being an oil painting and yet women were constantly attracted to him, supporting perhaps the theory that power is a great aphrodisiac. Pauline Grieve, a one-time organiser of the Liquor Reform Society who worked for him in several elections, sent birthday cards and Christmas greetings in florid language that would have brought a blush to the cheek of most men reading them: 'my very dearest friend, teacher, leader ... I am thinking of you all day and in all the days.' And again, this time with a letter headed 'Central Executive Australian Defence League': 'Your friendship is the greatest thing in my life ... but I am not certain that all is well between you and me ...', or on another occasion, 'I was born under a lucky star to have known and loved you'. In a letter recounting the bitter struggle she was having preparatory to separating from her husband, she wrote, 'I bless the day I met you'. But she always signed off her letters using her full name.

At one stage Hughes had her appointed to a job at £250 per annum with the Australian Democratic Front (ADF), 'front' being the appropriate word since its purpose was to support anticommunist propaganda, especially in the miners lodges. Mrs Grieve's salary was drawn from a confidential fund which, when it became public knowledge, produced an outcry: it was more party political than principled, it was said, and a royal commission was set up to look into the affair. Its eventual report exonerated Hughes from any wrongdoing in what came to be known as the 'Winkler affair' — so named after a former journalist on the old *Daily News*. Winkler had subsequently joined the Department of Information and then the PM's office before being drafted to run the fund. The enquiry had one victim, the luckless Winkler, who was sacked by Prime Minister Fadden.

And there was Ivie Price (who wrote the letter in Welsh to him), who was a regular correspondent, writing in 1949: 'Would your heart be strong enough if you saw me step off at Circular Quay one fine day? The Gowries are coming to stay near here ... I must now return to my fruits. Dame Mary will wonder what you are reading at the Breakfast table. I will write to her so jealousy doesn't set in ... your faithful Ivie.' She sent a get well telegram on 11 October 1952 after his breakdown in the House of Representatives from hypostatic pneumonia and a congested heart condition, saying: 'Get well soon. Shall I come out and nurse you?'

We also have Ursula Jones: 'My darling W.M. ... You and I ought to write to each other quite often and then we could publish them and call them the love letters of the little digger and make a lot of money ... All my love to you and the family ...'

In all the extant correspondence or stories about him and the testimony of numerous secretaries, many of whom were sacked by him, there is an uncanny absence of any rancour directed against him, no fulminations, no bitterness. Invariably we find only expressions of fondness and respect from female acquaintances and family members in his regard, although they were often aware of his many frailties in word and deed. Whether this was 'manoeuvring' or not, all the evidence suggests that he was inordinately attractive to women. One explanation may be that, given his lack of pulchritude, he was not seen initially as constituting any threat to women, who would perhaps have been on immediate guard with other overtly handsome men. They were comfortable in his presence, and, whatever charm he exhibited, women found it to be genuine and disinterested, while his physical features, rather than repelling, intrigued them. And although power may attract, a fascinating personality, genuine wit and telling turn of phrase can be equally devastating. The comments of two other of his secretaries bear this out. Marjorie Nichols, who worked for him between 1946 and 1950 and left for family reasons but remained good friends, wrote: 'Mr Hughes was not bad tempered but his lightning mind was always 3 jumps ahead of anyone else's and he was impatient that they weren't with him. I found him thoughtful of others and very kind.' Mrs Olga Northam, who worked for him off and on for some six years and was on duty during his final illness since his then regular secretary was on sick leave, wrote approvingly of his great attention to detail.

Chapter 6

Room at the top

Hughes became a minister in the three Labor administrations between 1908 and 1915, administrations which made notable progress in the development of Australia as a federated state, with the establishment of the Commonwealth Bank, introduction of a federal land tax, taking over responsibility for the Northern Territory (from South Australia) and preparatory work to establish a national capital. Prime Minister Fisher, like Hughes, had also emigrated to Australia and had been a train driver before entering politics, and would seem not to have jibbed at his deputy increasingly becoming the driving force in the government. Apart from exhibiting his usual vitality, Hughes was often the source of a spate of new legislative bills that hallmarked the government's performance in those years. While relations between the two men could not be described as particularly warm and they had numerous disagreements — Fisher much the more principled and less wily — nevertheless it would seem that common bonds of shared vicissitudes, physical disability (Fisher too, was partially deaf), political outlook and esteem remained throughout their long service in public life.

In the 1914 election, with hostilities having broken out in Europe, Labor was returned with a comfortable majority and a clear mandate to pursue the war vigorously. The Australian Imperial Force (AIF) was instituted and Australian and New Zealand troops despatched to the front. En route they encamped in Egypt, the bulk of the men at Mena near the pyramids where the Anzac appellation was first coined by an English clerk to expedite the sending of telegrams. One of the issues which attracted Hughes' particular attention was German control of the base metals industry — zinc, lead, copper — which was largely controlled by long-term contracts in the hands of German firms. With the help of industrialist W.S. Robinson,[1] whom Hughes later took with him to Europe, he persuaded Australian producers to break their contracts and make sure that they stayed outside German hands. He then set up the first Australian Metals Exchange to control exports.

Fisher resigned in October 1915 and Hughes was elected leader of the party unopposed, becoming Prime Minister. With barely a few months in office imperial issues beckoned and, accompanied by Mary and Helen, Hughes returned to Britain in 1916 having accepted Asquith's invitation to attend the Economic Conference of the Allies, the only Dominion leader to do so. Hughes stopped off in New Zealand for consultations with the New Zealand Prime Minister Massey and in Canada with Prime Minister Borden. In Canada he was given the signal honour of being made a member of the Canadian Privy Council on 18 February 1916. From a position of negligible influence 30 or so years earlier, Hughes believed that the Dominions had now acquired significant power, with the UK on the threshold of becoming 'first among equals' in their regard.[2]

From North America he travelled aboard an American steamer, the *Finland*, and reached England, docking in the Mersey on 6 March. He and his companions were met by Fisher, now Australian high commissioner to the UK. They stayed in London until August and were housed at the Cecil Hotel before moving to a private residence provided by the British Government. The following months became extremely busy for Hughes and he was able to revisit Llansantffraid accompanied by his wife and daughter, a nurse, and his secretary, a Mr Shepherd. Now that he was Prime Minister, the visit was well covered in the local press: the *Border Advertiser*, *Llandudno Advertiser* and the *Montgomery County Times*. He saw his relations, visited his mother's grave, and joined Lloyd George for a speech in Conway, passing through Rhuddlan and Llangollen on the way. One paper noted that he was 'not a complete stranger to the Welsh language'. He also returned to Llandudno, where the local cinema was showing Rider Haggard's *She* in five reels and a Buick car could be bought for £300. The visitors stayed at the St Georges Hotel, which had seen many famous people enter its doors, including Prince Bismarck. After a civic reception the party toured the areas Hughes remembered as a schoolboy, looking at Jackson's the Outfitters, hailing Jack Yr Ogof in Welsh, and meeting Jack Jones of the Miriam family, who had been a sailor and had visited Sydney. In an interview for the *Llandudno Advertiser* Hughes' preliminary remark was that he hoped it was not going to be in Welsh since if it was they would not get very far, maintaining that he could speak as much Welsh then as he ever could but that he had never been able to speak much. During the visit Shepherd his secretary fell the unfortunate victim of the wartime paranoia concerning spies and security, being arrested for taking a photograph of the Conway suspension bridge — forbidden by military rules. Hughes had to intervene personally to secure his release but the film was destroyed.

The Hughes boys

All three of Hughes' sons went to war, and it was Ernest, almost invariably referred to as Bill, who met his father on arrival in London wearing the uniform of the Australian Expeditionary Force. Bill had attended Hawkesbury Agricultural College in Richmond, New South Wales, as a resident student from May 1913 until he volunteered for active service in March 1916. During his three years at the college he studied in the Orchard Piggery and Trade shops and, according to the college principal, 'displayed considerable aptitude in each section and was noted for his activity, energy and willingness. He has a good all round knowledge of farm practice and livestock and in my opinion will prove a successful farmer.' An undated letter from Bill to his father when he was at Hawkesbury gave as good an indication of Hughes' parsimony (if not downright miserliness) as it did of Bill's forthrightness:

> some time since I wrote to you to get my sovereign off Mary ... I can't manage on 1/- a week. My list of things a week is:
>
> 1 tin carbolic
>
> haircut
>
> boots mended
>
> stamps
>
> soap
>
> bootlaces
>
> writing paper
>
> ties — I haven't got any
>
> I think 2/6 p.w. would be fair.

He had enlisted in March 1916 and embarked at Sydney on the *Benalla*, arriving in England on 12 May 1916. He was sent to the Grantham Transport School and, having successfully completed his training, was appointed driver with the 9th Machine Gun Company and sailed for France in November. In June the following year he was awarded the Military Medal for bravery in the field. A letter dated 26 November 1917 from him at the warfront in France to Charlie his younger brother read: 'I had word from Ethel ... the candle is getting very small ... Happy Xmas'. On 5 December, he wrote to his father that most of his fellow soldiers were in favour of conscription: 'We are out of the line for a short spell ... you say that probably the war will end next Autumn [a prophecy very close to what happened] ... trust that this will find you, Mary and dear little Helen in the best of health, Your loving son Bill'. A month later he had to forfeit six days' pay for being away without leave one day between 7 am and 10 am! On his enlistment form he gave his birthplace as Cumberland, Sydney, and his father's address as Cotham Rd, Kew. He described himself as being 5ft $7\frac{1}{2}$ ins tall with brown eyes and dark brown hair. On his demobilisation form he gave as his forwarding address that of his sister Ethel Bourke, Monaro, Middlehead Rd, Mosman, Sydney. He asked for early repatriation for 'urgent family reasons'.

Bill was mentioned in several letters sent by Keith Murdoch[3], who was sent to London in 1915 as managing editor of *The Sun* and the *Melbourne Herald* and was commissioned by Fisher and George Pearce (the Minister of Defence) to go to Gallipoli as a war correspondent. Having been pipped by C.E.W. Bean as the officially designated Australian press representative, Murdoch quickly become Hughes' unofficial bagman and confidant. He met Bill and wrote to Hughes that Bill had been introduced to Lloyd George and was well spoken of by his officers. He also referred to Bill having won the Military Medal and that his (Murdoch's) brother had won the Military Cross at the battle of Messines: 'He [Bill] liked the tinned fruit. He is doing well, is brave and fearless though somewhat haphazard, and is a great favourite with all except his superiors.' Murdoch followed this with a letter to General Monash on 24 July 1918 regarding Bill ('Driver Ernest Morris Hughes of the 9th Machine Gun Company'), suggesting he would make an excellent officer: 'I write this not in any way as a friend of Mr Hughes, who has said nothing to me on the subject. But the boy is a gallant and willing young soldier and has been in France with the 3rd Division for the last 15 months ... he has won the Military Medal for bravery in the field'. However, a later letter from Murdoch suggested that something had gone not quite according to plan: 'With regard to young Hughes: his father has now learnt the facts of the boy's failure and is naturally very vexed that the boy should not have done better justice to his upbringing. Any chance of him getting another chance? Re-entering cadet's school?' (Whatever the impact of this request, Bill was soon to return to civilian life with the cessation of hostilities.)

Brother Charles followed in Bill's footsteps in 1918, sailing from Sydney on the *Euripides* in May and arriving in France in August. His enlistment form gives his birthplace as Homebush, New South Wales, his profession as clerk and his height as 5ft $5\frac{3}{4}$ ins tall, adding that he had brown eyes, brown hair and fresh complexion. He gave his address as his parents' house, 145 Cotham Rd, Kew. He was attached to the recruitment Depot Batallion at Broadmeadows Camp with the rank of gunner. Charles, it seems, had the 'Hughes spirit': docking in New York on the way, he was given 68 hours' detention for wilful defiance of authority (breaking ranks).

From 1 February to the end of March 1919 he was granted paid leave from the army to study the textile trade in Bradford in England, 'where he underwent a very successful course in the treatment of wool and made very good progress'. Subsequently he worked with James Hill and Son in Bradford on wool classing for 6 shillings a day and was well regarded. He was discharged from the army on 3 January 1920, aged 20 years and five months, having completed his period of enlistment and having served 575 days overseas. On his demobilisation papers he gave Sassafras as his address for forwarding mail, having scratched out Cotham Rd, which suggests perhaps that his father had moved.

Arthur, Hughes' stepson, enlisted in the Australian Imperial Force in September 1918. On his application form he gave his birthplace as Melbourne, his height as 5ft $10\frac{1}{2}$ ins, his weight as 142 lbs, his address as 56 Market Street, Sydney, and his occupation as manufacturer's agent, noting also that he was married. The decision of the medical authority after his preliminary medical examination was that he be declared unfit for army service due to 'cardiac'. The medical officer at the Central Recruiting Depot concurred. However, the recruiting officer certified that he had accepted Arthur for enlistment. Though in the end he did not serve in the armed forces, he was given the rank of lieutenant and worked in the Contracts Branch of the Defence Department. Many years later, in a letter of 17 September 1939, Arthur offered his services to his father in World War II.

Annus mirabilis

Hughes became more and more lionised by the public in the United Kingdom, who warmed to his fresh rhetoric on what had to be done to win the war. In this he was strongly supported by Lord Northcliffe, the leading press baron of the day, who was liked by both Hughes and Murdoch for his directness: 'he knows what he wants and goes straight for it'. Hughes attended British Government cabinet meetings, was made a member of the privy council, met the political and establishment leaders of the day, dined at Windsor Castle with the King and Queen and was given a piece of embroidery done by the Queen herself. He travelled the country making stirring speeches: in Sheffield he was presented with a silver cup bowl and spoon for Helen. Hughes was made a freeman of several cities, including Cardiff, where he was welcomed as 'an illustrious son of Wales'. For the ceremony to receive the freedom of the city of London he invited six lecturers and students from his old Burdett-Coutts School. He also consolidated his good relations with Lloyd George (Lord Riddell[4] reported on a breakfast between the two men at which Hughes, commenting on the cabinet, said it was 'better to have fewer clever men and more ordinary ones. You'd get more done.') He managed to put the finishing touches on the settlement of the metals issue, as well as finding a solution for problems which had arisen back home in the sugar industry, notably in Queensland. (The then Queensland premier, T.J. O'Brien, who was no friend of Hughes, visited London at the same time and even stayed at the same hotel, but there is no evidence that the two met.)

Hughes made three trips to France, one as a member of the British delegation to attend the Economic Conference which held in Paris in June to determine what economic policies were to be adopted vis-a-vis Germany, and two to visit Australian troops of the AIF. An incident during one of the visits was recorded by Dame Enid Lyons in her book *Among The Carrion Crows*:[5] 'Hughes was at the front being briefed in whispers: the PM asked how far away the front was, half a mile came the response, so why were they whispering asked the PM, it transpiring that the soldier at the front had laryngitis and all others along the line had spoken in similarly hushed tones.' The title for her book came from Hughes' words to her when she entered Parliament in 1943 as the first lady member of the lower house: 'You sat like a bird of paradise among the carrion crows.'

Billy Hughes

During his time in the UK Hughes was instrumental in arranging for the purchase of 15 cargo vessels urgently needed to transport a bountiful wheat harvest from Australia to the UK. Percy Deane, who became Hughes' private secretary and subsequently head of the Prime Minister's Office and was, according to observers, the only person who could really handle him, noted that this had occasioned words with Lloyd George since Hughes had proceeded with the purchase against the wishes of the British Government. On his return to Australia, Hughes commanded that a number of wooden bay and cargo steamers be built. They were constructed in the United States and became the nucleus of the Commonwealth Shipping Line and launched an indigenous Australian shipbuilding industry. For many years they were referred to as 'Billy Hughes ships'. He was abetted in the transaction by W.S. Robinson and Keith Murdoch.

Murdoch's reporting during the war, though often more polemical than an unvarnished account of the facts, was nevertheless highly effective. As early as September 1915 he wrote to George Pearce (who was perhaps Hughes' greatest ally in politics), pleading earnestly that old Brigadiers should not be sent to the peninsular: 'Without doubt some of our Brigadiers have cost as many lives through their ignorance and through their inadaptability to these extraordinary conditions. Oh, there is a lot of murder through incapacity.' It was his report on the Dardanelles situation that rushed him into fame (for some) or notoriety (for others). Lloyd George saw that the report was circulated to the cabinet, promising that the Ministry of Defence would take action on it. As an immediate result, Maurice Hankey, Secretary to the Cabinet, was despatched to the Dardanelles and the Dardanelles Commission set up. The commission reported on 5 February 1917 after meeting for 43 days, and its recommendations led to the withdrawal of troops and the saving of countless lives.

During Hughes' voyage home on the *Euripides* in June 1916, where, according to an old digger, he shared many yarns on the salon deck, he wrote to Murdoch, saying 'I miss you dreadfully and this is the very best compliment I can pay you and the clearest evidence of how much I value your friendship', and upbraiding him for addressing Hughes as 'Prime Minister'. Hughes added: 'The Party meeting is fixed for the 24th, the Parliament meeting the 30th ... I am neither hopeful nor hopeless but I shall do what I think is right' (apropos of the imminent battle over conscription of troops to serve overseas). A month later he wrote to Murdoch from Durban, South Africa, 'I wouldn't live in this country if I could help it. They are torn by factions and impaled upon the point of snobbery. Racial hatred and class bitterness, plus the coloured labour syndrome make a first class imitation of hell.' As ever, Hughes here demonstrated his capacity for going directly to the nub of an issue.

Chapter 7
Conscription and the birth of nationalism

Billy Hughes reached Australia in July 1916 and was caught up immediately in a storm of his own making: the first referendum on conscription, called for October. Labor Party and public opinion in Australia on his return was very different from what it had been at the war's outset. In a document in 1914, with Fisher the party leader and Prime Minister, the position of the Labor Party was stated thus:

> Our interest and our very existence are bound up with those of the Empire. In time of war, half measures are worse than none. If returned with a majority we shall pursue with the utmost rigour and determination every course necessary for the defence of the Commonwealth and the Empire in any and every contingency.

By 1916, however, that commitment had been negated by the two intervening years of strife. The issue was perhaps the watershed in Australian politics: it divided the country on largely sectarian fault lines, split the Labor Party (consigning it to pasture for 14 years), and saw the grossest propaganda from both sides. There was claim and counterclaim, exaggeration after exaggeration, encomium after encomium, engendering huge and lasting bitterness and hatred in which no person's reputation was sacrosanct. According to some press reports, an attempt was made on Hughes' life when an intruder allegedly entered his home at Kew, though *The Worker* pooh-poohed the suggestion, maintaining that the person who had been noticed near the house was the milkman.

Billy Hughes

In all this there remains a fundamental unanswered question: why did Hughes decide on a referendum to determine the issue? Why did this 'ruthless, shrewd and artful' politician and statesman choose such an instrument when he did not need to? Conscription became law in New Zealand, Canada and the UK and later even in the United States — decisions taken by the governments of the day. And Hughes could have done the same via the War Precautions Act, though there remains a doubt that he would have got it through the Senate. For the subsequent second referendum he could even have forced it through with his majority in Parliament. The letter to Murdoch showed quite clearly that it was not because he thought the issue beyond doubt; rather the contrary, that it was a highly risky enterprise. He was well aware too of the likely divide in the country: the political situation in Ireland was something he followed closely, and he would have appreciated well the negative impact the Easter Uprising in Dublin earlier in the year would have had on the Australian-Irish, however much their sympathies had earlier been with their fellow Catholics in France and Belgium. He had no illusions either as to the impact on his party, knowing full well how significant a proportion of it was of Irish background.

Bonar Law, who had once described Hughes as a 'Lloyd George only more so', was briefly the UK Prime Minister after Lloyd George, and Secretary of State for the Colonies under Asquith. He received a letter from Murdoch at *The Times* offices in London of 20 November 1916, noting that voting in the field among the soldiers on conscription was running strongly against, and that Hughes had not allowed this to be made public, but that, if the new division which had just arrived at Salisbury Plain and the troops in Egypt were taken into account, there was a margin of 10 000 in favour of conscription overall.

Hughes sent a secret cable to Lloyd George on 30 December 1916: 'There is war to the knife between the old section of the Labor Party and my section. The old Labor Party ... embraces two distinct factions: one syndicalists, two Irish. Two is the keystone of the sectional arch. Cut that away and the whole opposition crumbles.' The Irish population of Australia was around 25 per cent (not less than 80 per cent of which were in the labour movement), and the overwhelming majority of the Irish at present were hostile to the policy necessary for the effective prosecution of the war. Defeat in the referendum was mainly due to Irish opposition and had been very bitter. The Irish question was now an imperial question. Hughes, in a letter at the time, noted that there cannot be Imperial unity as long as a disunited Ireland exists.

Lloyd George replied that he could not personally solve the Irish question, and any settlement had to be on the basis of an agreement between the leaders of the North and South. Hughes returned to the theme in a further note of 17 August 1917 to Lloyd George: 'The Irish question is at the bottom of all our difficulties in Australia. They the Irish have captured the political machinery of the Labor organisations assisted by the syndicalists. One of their Archbishops is a Sinn Feiner — I am trying to make up my mind whether I should prosecute him for statements hindering security or deport him.' This was Archbishop Mannix, one of the bitterest opponents of conscription, particularly in the second referendum campaign. Holman commented of him that he 'had not long arrived from Ireland [and] was the victim of a strange incapacity to "keep his block" when in front of an applauding crowd'; he perceptively added: 'There is always a prejudice in Australia against sacerdotal politics. This prejudice the Archbishop did his uttermost to arouse and justify ... like Mr Hughes himself [he] was as indifferent to the claims of accuracy or moderation as himself. Mr Hughes has a temperament which is somehow unfitted for the winning of plebiscites.'

Not all people of Irish extraction, or all Catholics, were in favour of Mannix. One W.J. Toohey wrote to Hughes after a speech he had given in Bendigo: 'heartiest congratulations. I am a Catholic by birth and conviction and I consider David Mannix is a positive danger to our national well-being ... a political mountebank masquerading as a priest.' The Prince of Wales wrote to congratulate Hughes on 'your utterances against that ... dangerous Mannix'. (An interesting gloss on his relations with Mannix was how feelings between the two men mellowed considerably in later years, with exchanges of Christmas and birthday cards. Apart from the inevitable dimming of passion with increasing age and separation from those turbulent years, it was their common position against contraception that assuaged their mutual dislike of each other. Mannix telegraphed on 3 October 1941: 'Extremely grateful for your messages and for your prompt and decisive public statement [on the evils of contraception].')[1]

Murdoch's view was that the conscription issue had been forced on Hughes by a gang-up of the Australian-Irish and the conservative elements in the trade unions — united in their dislike of the English. Other factors which held sway were: the belief that Australia had 'done her bit', that she had to look more at Asia, the farmers' need for labour, the argument that the British authorities didn't understand the Australian soldier, and that Australia should have had its own command. There was, too, a strong anti-conscription tone in the soldiers' letters home from the front which increased as the war dragged on and more and more casualties were reported.

But these elements, even in combination, are not enough to explain why Hughes opted for referenda. One clue might reside in his legal background and respect for the law. He had hitherto been somewhat lukewarm as regards conscription as a principle and had spoken against it. Back in 1907, speaking in London, he had argued that a voluntary system was to be preferred for armed service overseas, which had been the traditional British practice and remained so until 1916. He was a constitutionalist and, whatever machinations or duplicity he manifested during his political career, there are few traces of him abandoning his respect for the primacy of the law or the pre-eminence of the constitutional basis of the democratic state. Holman was insightful in this respect: he believed that Hughes genuinely felt that the War Reparations Act did not give him the legal right to conscript, 'for Mr Hughes had not up to then developed the blood lust for autocracy which he afterwards achieved'.[2]

The answer perhaps lies in the fact that Hughes was more aware than most that the Allies could lose the war, and it was not merely a case of having been suborned or seduced by the adulation he had been subjected to during his sojourn in Britain; a possible victory by Germany was no idle fancy. Hughes believed that, despite the horrors of Gallipoli and Pozieres, the prospect of German ascendancy was abhorrent, with the German possessions in the Pacific, in Australia's immediate hinterland, constituting a real threat and a worse prospect to contemplate than sending more young men to the trenches. Kim Beazley, writing in the *Canberra Times* in February 1966 saw it differently, lamenting Hughes' failure to exploit his standing in the UK and persuade the British Government to get rid of General Haig and stem the appalling loss of life: 'he [Hughes] should have been a force for the intelligent use of manpower.'

A necessary war

There is a developing, revisionist view of World War I which perhaps needs greater airing: that the inherited wisdom that it was an unnecessary war, with needless slaughter and incompetent officers, is a gross distortion of the truth. An articulate proponent of this view is Gordon Corrigan,[3] who argues with an abundance of corroborative detail that Germany had been planning a war of aggression against France, Russia and Britain since 1910 and that Britain's entry into the war was inevitable if Germany's aims of territorial aggrandisement in Europe and overseas were to be defeated. As for the view that the war was one of 'lions led by donkeys', Corrigan is convincing in showing that, overall, the war was not conducted ineptly and that Haig, far from being the incompetent blackguard of popular legend, was the person 'who transformed a tiny volunteer British Army into a professional force capable of defeating Germany'. He also shows that the attrition rate for officers relative to total numbers was greater than for other ranks. Between 1914 and 1918, 12 per cent of other ranks were killed compared with 17 per cent of officers, and 200 British generals were killed, wounded or captured.

A cable from Murdoch expressed that the prospect of defeat for the Allies was greater in the early months of 1918, which accounted for 25 per cent of Australia's casualties throughout the war. Hughes may have believed that his own personal magnetism and standing with the electors was enough to secure the positive outcome he wanted from the second referendum — an example of the self-deception that can assail even the cleverest of statesmen who have enjoyed prolonged periods of power. According to the historian of the Australian Home Front during the war, Professor Ernest Scott, 'In inviting a democracy to conscript itself, Hughes attempted to do something that had never been done anywhere in the annals of war'. What ensued, almost with the inevitability of a Greek tragedy, became one of the bitterest occasions in Australian political history and coloured perceptions of Hughes ever after. Despite his efforts to keep the party together there was simply no majority possible for conscription after the Labor caucus instructed all its members to work against the referendum, with expulsion for any member working in its favour. Caucus duly met and passed a motion of no confidence in Hughes, at which point he rose to his feet, gathered his papers and — with a 'Let all who support me follow me' — stalked out of the room with only 23 out of 65 following him. It is a considerable irony that, even if he had carried the day and won the referendum, it is doubtful that many more men would have been drafted than went voluntarily.

After the defeat of the first conscription referendum by 60 000 votes, Murdoch wrote to Hughes, 'I am confident that you will form a coalition and will proceed with another test of the people's wishes'. He concluded the letter: 'Have you booked me an Australian wife? If I'm not knocked by a shell or a bullet, I will claim her one day.' Hughes replied after the split of the Labour Party: 'Do not think that the referendum is the cause of this unhappy division, it is not, it is only the occasion for it.' On 28 November 1916 Hughes further wrote: 'My dear Keith, Your letter hailing me as King Bill just to hand. "King" — I'm a poor worm: worse than a worm for I do not know how to turn.' Murdoch returned to the theme of wife-searching the following July: 'Can't you help me by wooing a matronly Australian mate for me. Your courting is irresistible.' Hughes responded: 'Helen grows with such amazing rapidity both in wisdom and stature — and her flow of conversation is such — that if you will only restrain your matrimonial ambitions for a little while you will when you return fall a victim to her manifold charms.' In September 1917, Hughes promised to get an Australian girl for him: 'In fact there is a very fine one not too far from here who has just gone with Mary looking for a nurse. She is sound in wind and limb, temper (I think) all right, age about 22/3. Shall I book the order?' Whether the lady in Hughes' mind was Elizabeth Green, who Sir Keith married in 1928, is not known.

In the same letter Hughes added that 'Adela Pankhurst is making herself a d...d nuisance and I really do not know what to do with the little devil. I hate punishing women but I fear I shall have to deport her.' This was the daughter of Emmeline Pankhurst, whom Hughes had a lot of time for; her daughter, however, was being a nuisance in Australia, demonstrating against the war effort. What he did do was put her in jail. (She had recently married a militant trade unionist, Tom Walsh, Secretary of the Seamen's Union, and would in later years become a founder member of the Communist Party of Australia, in 1920, and be interned for advocacy of peace with Japan, in 1941–43.) Her activities in Australia in 1917 were greatly deplored by her mother, who was strongly supportive of what Hughes was doing. In an interview many years later Adela was reported as saying that she bore him no malice and indeed admired him as a man who acted without personal ill-feeling.

Hughes recounted some difficulties he was having with Australia House in London: 'Fisher is evidently hostile to me personally: he has not sent me a line even officially since I left England.' He had heard, too, that Murdoch was considering giving up journalism for a job in Australia House. Hughes urged him not to: 'you were made for your present job'. In the same letter, commenting on honours, he said he was basically opposed to them other than for service in the field or recommended by the Commonwealth Government. A reply from Murdoch made it perfectly clear that he, Murdoch, was in no way interested in a job at the High Commission. A further letter from Murdoch came, warmly recommending Charles Lloyd Jones, managing director of David Jones and director of *The Sun*, to Hughes' attention.

At the subsequent election Hughes, having joined the rump of old Labor combined with the Liberals, won handsomely and reflected: 'what amazing changes the churn of circumstance cast forth. A few months earlier the leader of a great party, then every man's hand against him and now the leader of the greatest party ever gathered together in the history of the commonwealth with 77 seats', though he added that he was, 'mindful as ever of the pregnant saying that him that thinketh he should stand, take heed lest he fall'. And fall he did, losing the second referendum, with the consequent letter to Murdoch expressing considerable bitterness. He had considered complete withdrawal from public life but the party had asked him to remain with a vote of 65 to 2. A later cable had Murdoch expressing much concern over German reports that they believed a decisive victory for them was in sight.

Attacks on Hughes and his conduct during the war came from many sources. Some attacks were virulent, especially, as one would have expected, from the left-wing and trade union press. Labor supporters in particular felt betrayed, and the sense of betrayal passed on to future generations. Apart from Hughes' defection, however, Labor's woes were exacerbated by the loss of many of its leading lights in the early years of the 1920s: William Higgs, a former Commonwealth treasurer; Hugh Mahon, expelled from Parliament for allegedly seditious utterings concerning British wrongs committed against Ireland and the Irish; T.J. Ryan, who died in 1921; and Frank Tudor, who died only six months later. One letter, which epitomised a sometimes vitriolic tone, included: 'As for Billy Hughes he lost the chance of his lifetime when he failed to die of that English cold he caught'.[4] According to his attackers, Hughes' campaign for conscription had been disastrous for Australia, 'a fatuous and cowardly policy', and his so-called successes (reorganising the metal industry, establishing the wheat and wool pools) had been the work of others: 'he was full of florid rhetoric — A calamitous mountebank';[5] 'Hughes makes it a rule never to see more than one side of a case at a time, though he may see all sides in turn. He is more the slave than the master of his own rhetoric.'[6] Holman wrote of his campaigning: 'Mr Hughes' fighting speeches were often on the lines of the celebrated recipe for a love letter, started without knowing what was going to be said and finished without knowing what had been said.' And on another occasion: 'Mr Hughes has probably never stated a case quite candidly or fully in his life.'

Command of Australian troops was exercised initially by the English General Birdwood, with whom Hughes exchanged warmish regards over many years, as did Mary with the general's wife. Birdwood's was a hugely difficult job, with Australian troops based in France, training in England and fighting in Egypt and Palestine. Later he became Officer Commanding the Fifth British Army when the Australian-born Sir John Monash became GOC (General Officer Commanding) of the Australian Corps British Armies France, having previously commanded the 4th Australian Infantry Brigade, which had served throughout the Gallipoli campaign, and the Third Australian Division. Of Russian-Jewish origins, Monash was a meticulous planner and became very well regarded by his British counterparts as well as by his own men. His appointment as commander of the Australian Corps was supported by Birdwood and Haig but opposed at the time both by Bean, who betrayed a nasty streak of anti-Semitism, and Murdoch. Both conspired to use their influence with Hughes to block Monash's appointment but failed to do so, Hughes preferring to accept the views of his commanders in the field as well as his own judgement.

The Little Digger

In April 1918, Hughes returned to Europe via the United States, where he saw President Wilson and where Dame Mary launched the steamship *Bundarra* in Seattle. During the trip he referred to the need for Australia to establish a representative office in the US, noting that all South American countries were represented. Arriving in the UK some days later than the official party, having missed his boat connection in New York, he was given a house in Chalk Farm by the British Government, whereas his deputy, and Minister for the Navy, Sir Joseph Cook, stayed at The Savoy. Others in the Australian party of nine included Percy Deane, Sir Robert Garran (who later was to become attorney-general and be much respected by all sides of politics), and John Latham, Naval Staff Officer to the Minister of Defence, whose subsequent career included stints as Deputy Prime Minister and Chief Justice of the High Court. Latham was antipathetic to Hughes but seemed to have a sneaking admiration for his

Billy Hughes

PM's bulldog qualities, though not his brashness or his perceived cavalier treatment of Cook. He also shared the same anxieties as Hughes regarding Japan's intentions in the Pacific and it was he who delivered the formula for the so-called 'C' mandate, which gave Australia control over New Guinea and the islands south of the equator. Hughes would have preferred outright annexation and acquiesced to the C compromise only on the understanding that it amounted to the equivalent of a 999-year lease.

Hughes had continued to make visits to the front in 1918 and 1919. At one point, Augustus John, another fellow Welshman, came to Paris to paint his portrait. On seeing the painting Hughes said to the great man, 'I've never done you any harm'. 'Why do you say that?' queried John, 'because you've made me a cross between a Red Indian and a Whitechapel Jew', said Hughes. John then tore up the first canvas and started again. Hughes also visited Lille in northern France in March 1919 and at Lyons made a speech in French, which not unsurprisingly was well regarded and well reported in the French press. He spent three days with Percy Deane going to Hamel, Villers Bretonneux, along the Somme to Bray, Clery, Mont St Quentin and Peronne, viewing the ground ploughed by shells, guns standing still and trenches full of equipment abandoned by retreating Germans. He saw the huge gun captured at Chignolles by the Australian Third Batallion — 15 metres long and with the aperture of the gun barrel measuring 380 centimetres, on which he engraved his initials. At Bray he spoke to more than a thousand soldiers in front of the very picturesque church and announced that he had negotiated a deal whereby the troops would all soon return to Australia for leave.

Unlike the British and the French, who maintained a policy throughout the war of shooting deserters, Hughes ensured that this would not be the fate of Australian deserters on the Western Front. Corrigan writes that, of the 5 million soldiers who passed through the British Army in the course of the war, 2400 were sentenced to death but 90 per cent were pardoned or had their sentences commuted.[7] One-hundred-and-thirteen Australian soldiers were sentenced to death, but the power to confirm a death sentence rested with the governor-general, who invariably reduced the sentence to one of imprisonment. He also maintains that Australian generals would have dearly wished on occasion to shoot some of their men whose 'superb fighting record was counterbalanced by appalling discipline'. The Australian soldier was nine times more liable to serve a term of imprisonment than his British counterparts, the sentences being handed down by Australian courts martial composed of Australian officers. Earle Page, in his tribute in Parliament on Hughes' death, acknowledged that although Australian forces in World War I were part of the Allied Command it was largely Hughes who ensured that they retained their separate Australian identity and that ultimate control of their welfare rested with the Australian Government. It was also the 'Little Digger' who introduced the first repatriation measure.

The Imperial War Conference commenced on 12 June 1918 and went on until 27 July, held on alternate days to meetings of the Imperial War Cabinet. Both were attended by Hughes, continuing when the War Conference was reconvened from October to December. During this period there was a discernible growth in criticism, both in parts of the Australian and British press, for what they perceived to be clear evidence of a growing autocracy in Hughes' demeanour, attitude and utterance. *The Times* of London wrote on 26 November 1918 of criticisms in Australia that Hughes was making too much of the wounds to his *amour propre*, and attacked his thirst for publicity and contemptuous disregard for Joseph Cook. Hughes always referred to his deputy as 'Joe', who was always joyless according to some contemporaries. Hughes recalled an occasion in Paris when, after the Armistice, he went out on the town while Cook went to preach in a Methodist church. 'How he found a Methodist church in Paris is beyond me', said Hughes. There is no evidence that Cook himself was much perturbed by his PM's disdain, and he remained a loyal supporter of Hughes throughout his career. The London *Daily Telegraph* followed *The Times* report with an account of Hughes' expulsion from the Wharf Labourers Union over conscription. He was also removed from the presidency of the Waterside Workers Federation and commented to one journalist that he had conveyed this news to his baby daughter, Helen, who said, 'Goo goo'. 'Well you don't seem to care a damn so neither do I', said her father.

This notwithstanding, Holman wrote that Hughes had been the right man at the right time in 1916: 'far sighted, determined, persuasive, unscrupulous at need ... a capacity to see a dozen moves ahead'.[8] For Holman, one needed a long spoon to sup with Hughes politically (it is probable that Hughes took the title for his book, *Policies and Powers*, from one of Holman's chapters also thus entitled). According to Holman, Hughes was the brilliant opportunist, the leading light in the Labor Government and the originator of the constitutional amendment to give the Federal Parliament control of all domestic industry and commerce. He acknowledged Hughes' strengths but also his weaknesses, and the picture he gives of him whiffs of verisimilitude:

> No man was ever perhaps so entirely the architect of his own fortune as Mr Hughes. Other men owe their rise to happy chance or to the enthusiasm of adoring disciples. The lucky accidents in Mr Hughes' career have been far fewer than the blows of circumstance ... he has never been enshrined in the hearts of the community. When most admired he has been least beloved. The softer emotions, if he did evoke them, would be an embarrassment to him. Men have accepted him as an indispensable and invaluable rather than as a lovable personality.

Chapter 8
The Peace Conference

The Peace Conference was convened on 12 January 1919, with the British Empire being accorded 14 representatives including two from Australia, Hughes and Cook. For Murdoch, Hughes' huge contribution to Australia's future at the conference was the removal of the German menace from the South Pacific. Although failing to secure outright annexation of the ex-German territories by Australia, getting his country mandatory authority over the islands situated between the equator and 8 degrees latitude South and between 14.1 E and 159.25 longitude was almost as good. For Holman, Hughes' major achievement was winning the battle to prevent a racial equality clause being included in the covenant of the resulting treaty, a clause which had been much lobbied for by the Japanese Government. In this regard the position which Hughes defended vigorously and which he conveyed privately and publicly to the Japanese delegation was that: 'there was no objection to a declaration of racial equality in the Covenant [to the eventual treaty] provided that it was stated in precise and unambiguous terms that this did not confer any right to enter into Australia except as and to the extent that its Government might from time to time determine.' To Baron Makino of the Japanese delegation he said that their ideals, institutions and standards were not 'ours. I did not say that ours were any greater or better, but only that they were different.' Hughes remained convinced that a racial equality clause allowing people of all countries to pass freely into the territories of all other members of the League of Nations would have seen the Japanese flood into Papua New Guinea, other Pacific islands and Australia. Holman wrote in this respect: 'Had he lost his fight for the Mandate [Australian responsibility for New Guinea] and had he yielded to the powerful demand for the inclusion of the Racial Equality Clause in the Covenant of the League of Nations it is more than doubtful if Australia could have been successfully defended in the last war.'

In the light of the events of January, February and March 1942, many regarded Hughes' words then as prophetic. If Australia had been denied control of Guinea, Japan's first 'treacherous thrust' would have been at the Australian mainland; the opposite view was held by others such as Justice Pal, the Indian judge on the War Crimes Tribunal in 1948, who regarded Hughes' stand over both the mandate issue and the racial equality clause as thoroughly irresponsible. In Pal's view, this had led to Japan entering World War II. Baron Makino's subsequent grave warning that public opinion in Japan would hold Australia accountable for failure to secure an amendment in the covenant providing for racial equality was widely quoted in the Australian press. Meanwhile, the Japanese press continually referred to Hughes' utterances as characterised by the most pronounced racial prejudice and by an assumption of racial superiority of the white race over the races of the Far East. It is tempting to speculate on what effect this had on Baron Makino, who, subsequent to his return to Japan, became Lord Privy Seal and a close adviser to Emperor Hirohito in the years leading to Japan's attack on Pearl Harbor.

Percy Deane, who was appointed secretary to the Australian delegation at the Peace Conference, had become Hughes' private secretary in 1918 and later headed the Prime Minister's Department before retiring in 1936. Some years after the Peace Conference, an article in the *Chicago Tribune* aroused Deane's ire in accusing Hughes of having given the islands north of the equator to the Japanese. Deane riposted that the issue had been quite clear: the problem at Versailles was not Hughes but Wilson, who in his view had the preconceived prejudice of a college professor; Hughes was only given one hour's warning by phone to go down and put Australia's case before the big four (Wilson, Lloyd George, French Prime Minister Georges Clemenceau, and Italian leader

Vittorio Orlando): 'I have one hour to prepare the entire case for Australia. I know what Wilson wants. He wants the ex-German territories to form the basis of his non-existent League. Australia won't get New Guinea except under mandate from the League of Nations. Get your notebook: "New Guinea lies like a rampart across our Northern shores. In our hands it is a guarantee of our safety; in the hands of a potential enemy it is a grave and ever present menace".' According to Deane it was at this meeting that the most famous bout between Hughes and Wilson occurred:

Wilson: 'But after all you speak for only five million people'.

Hughes: 'I speak for sixty thousand dead. For how many do you speak?'

This occasioned a major disagreement with Lloyd George. Hughes' account of their altercation was published in the *Ballarat Courier* many years later, as well as in *The Cambrian News* and *Welsh Farmer's Gazette*:

> At the Peace Conference after World War 1 the Imperial Cabinet [basically the British Cabinet and the Prime Ministers of the Dominions] gathered one morning to consider the position created by President Wilson's ultimatum that if I insisted upon control over New Guinea being given to Australia he would leave the Conference and go back to America. Lloyd George was much upset and said that he would be no party to breaking up the Conference, and that I could not look to Britain for support. As I believed that the control was vital to the very existence of Australia I told him just where I stood in the matter — and that whether Wilson went or stayed Australia must have the mandate. Naturally Mr Lloyd George was incensed by my mulish obstinacy and did not spare his criticism. And of course I gave as good as I received — and so it went on until at last goaded beyond endurance I threw English to the winds and fell back on our own more beautiful tongue — which is rich in expletives calculated to pierce the most pachydermous hides. Lloyd George looked at me, his eyes blazing and 'Et tu Brute' struggled for utterance between his lips — And saying that he was going to the Council of the Four and asking Bonar Law and Lord Hankey to try and find a formula that would satisfy me, hurried away. Bonar Law and Hankey got to work — while the rest of the Cabinet sat twiddling their

thumbs wondering what on earth was going to be the outcome of this most unseemly incident. I waited a while and then turned to Bonar Law and asked him how he and Hankey were progressing. Bonar Law looked at me with a twinkle in his eye and said: 'Hankey and I were wondering, what it was you said to Lloyd George'. 'Oh' I said 'I don't know but in English I suppose I told him to go to the devil.' 'Oh' said Bonar, 'it sounded much worse than that.'

Hughes did not help matters when, in replying to Wilson's request for his agreement on adding a clause on freedom of opinion to allow the natives free access to missionaries of any denomination, he said: 'By all means Mr President. I understand these poor people sometimes go for months without half enough to eat.' Everyone laughed except Wilson, according to Hughes. The *Herald* reported the incident slightly differently: that Wilson wanted to hold a referendum among the native inhabitants, to which Hughes had replied incredulously that some of those people ate each other. On another occasion the *Herald* wrote that, if a plebiscite had been held, the electoral officers would have been eaten by the voters.

Hughes' views of Australia's role in the Pacific were a combination both of political sensitivity, racism and wide reading, including letters from correspondents who wrote to him on this and related issues. One such was journalist W.H. Donald, based in Peking, who had previously been editor of the *Far Eastern Review* and had also worked for the *Manchester Guardian* and the *New York Herald*. Hughes became persuaded that the future of Australia was closely bound up with the development of the countries of the Pacific Ocean, that Japan was trying to control China and become overlord of all Asiatic countries including India, and that her aim was to attack and conquer Australia and resist the 'white world'. He believed that the UK was obliged to support Japan's 21 demands in respect of China to keep her on the Allied side in the war. Donald had written: 'We betrayed China to assuage the blood-lust of Japan and by doing that we have to an extent antagonised the Chinese and placed a whip in the hands of Japan which may in the end scourge us'. He added that Japan was as unscrupulous as she was ambitious —

'in methods and mentality Japan is Prussian' — and that the 'white races' had to insist on a square deal being given to China: 'She has the makings of a great democratic nation and is the greatest market in the world and will always be a curb on the ambitions of Japan.'

Hughes was much concerned with the Anglo-Japanese pact. Signed in 1911, the pact was to last for a ten-year period and was much favoured by Hughes, who lobbied hard with the British Government for its renewal. He had a keen appreciation that it was essential to keep Japan on side during the war to ensure that she was not an imminent threat to Australia. One letter to Hughes argued perceptively: 'In renewing the Anglo-Japanese pact it should be borne in mind that there is a good deal more than a mere off-chance of America drifting into war with Japan within the next ten years, further more in dealing with the Japanese Foreign Office one was not always dealing with a principal ... The military chiefs have a policy of their own which is often in conflict with that of the Foreign Office and in the last resort it is the policy of the military chiefs which prevails.'

Others wrote, in similar vein, that:

- Australasia could resist Japanese pretensions to free ingress only so long as Japan did not command the Pacific.
- If the UK could maintain a fleet equivalent to the Japanese navy in the latitude of Singapore, Japanese sea power would be restricted to Japanese waters and the British position in the Indian Ocean and Australasia secured.
- America was not capable of waging a naval war — an incapacity which combined with arrogance towards the Japanese on trans-Pacific questions was precipitating a war for which the US was not prepared. The failure of the five-power naval conference in 1936, resulting from the refusal to grant Japan parity with the British and the United States navies, saw this fear fulfilled.

Various references were made to Hughes' first meeting with Clemenceau at the Peace Conference. Reith Kirkaldy in a letter of 28 February 1929 quoted Churchill's story in *Aftermath* of Clemenceau allegedly saying, 'I understand Mr Hughes that in your early days you were a cannibal', to which Hughes is supposed to have replied, 'I assure you Mr Clemenceau, that is somewhat of an exaggeration'. Clemenceau was perhaps referring to Hughes' rumbustious, take-no-prisoners approach, which so got up the nose of Wilson but delighted 'Tiger' Clemenceau. At one point an exasperated Wilson addressed Hughes thus: 'Do you disagree with the considered opinion of these international experts?' Hughes: 'Just exactly that.' Another version had Wilson saying: 'Do I understand that Australia in the face of the wishes of the world would insist upon having her own way?', with Hughes replying, 'Yes that's about it'.

For Hughes, Wilson was 'as humourless as the Great Pyramid ... as impassive as an undertaker at a pauper's funeral'. For Wilson, Hughes was a 'pestiferous varmint'. In the US presidential election of 1916 Wilson had fought his campaign on the basis of keeping the US out of the war. His Republican opponent, strangely enough, was another Hughes — Charles Evan Hughes[1] — who, when he became Secretary of State to President Harding in 1921, was faced with the daunting task of negotiating a separate peace treaty with Germany after the US refusal to sign the Versailles Treaty. The antipathy between Hughes and Wilson did not extend to other members of the American delegation; he established good relations with Bernard Baruch, for example, who became one of the foremost advisers to a succession of American presidents and who sent a floral tribute for Hughes' funeral. The legal adviser to the US delegation at the conference was John Foster Dulles, whom Hughes met up with a dozen years later during his visit to America. Of Hughes' performance at the Peace Conference, a New York newspaper wrote that Hughes was afforded as much deference as the representatives of the big powers and for years afterwards remained for many leading American politicians 'the doughty defender of democracy'.

The friendship with Clemenceau, and also General Botha from South Africa, flourished during the Australian's prolonged stay at the Majestic Hotel in the Avenue Kleber near the Arc de Triomphe in Paris. Hughes recalled the incident during the conference when a demented youth

The Peace Conference

shot Clemenceau through the lung and Clemenceau, later intervening with the authorities to save the boy from the guillotine, returned to the conference unable to speak. Of Hughes, Clemenceau wrote: 'in the first rank I ought to have placed Mr Hughes, the notable delegate from Australia, with whom we had to talk through an electrophone, getting in return symphonies of good sense'. Hughes would have shared Clemenceau's view that war was too serious a matter to entrust to military men. A letter from an E.B. Jones in Wales — ending 'Hir oes ag Hapusrwydd' ('A long life and happiness') — reminded Hughes of an anecdote from the Peace Conference when someone said to Clemenceau that he'd seen a billboard announcing 'train disaster' and another 'train accident', and wondered what the difference was, with Clemenceau replying: 'If Wilson fell into a well it would be an accident but if someone rescued him it would be a disaster.' (A similar joke was doing the rounds in Margaret Thatcher's time.)

Hughes warmed to other players at the conference, including Paderewski the Polish Foreign Minister and concert pianist; he was, Hughes said, of 'leonine mane but didn't act as their spokesman' (whose name was Domonski). At one point during the negotiations concerning the vexed issue of the Polish corridor, Deane recounted how the various suggestions made produced a map criss-crossed with lines reminiscent of a musical score, which occasioned Hughes to suggest that it might make more sense if Paderewski took it home and played it on the piano. Hughes also liked Sonnino from Italy, a very gifted linguist whom Hughes spoke to in Welsh and who greatly astonished Hughes by repeating his words perfectly. He subsequently learned that Sonnino's mother was in fact Welsh. He was not too enamoured of Smuts, writing to General Sir Ronald Wingate many years later that: 'General Smuts was always on the side of the downtrodden except when they got between the wind and his nobility — as in the case of the Indians in South Africa when they received short shrift.'

Hughes' propensity for going it alone and ignoring the ordinary and established norms of cabinet responsibility were well established, and his boast that he had 'ruled Australia with a pen' was by then common knowledge. However, in regard to his conduct at the conference an examination of the exchange of telegrams between Hughes and William Watt (the Acting Prime Minister in Australia during the conference) indicate that, although it took some three to four days between despatch and receipt of telegrams, there was consultation, even if it was largely Hughes who took the decisions. Hughes cabled home regularly from November 1918 to May 1919 outlining the key developments in the negotiations, the various points at issue, and his insistence on defending Australian interests. One of his strongest protests concerned Wilson's '14 points', which were to be the basis for peace terms; it was not so much the content he objected to as the fact that Australia had not been consulted in their regard, nor had they been discussed by the Imperial War Cabinet. One of these cables, of 26 January, puts it succinctly: 'Wilson is in trouble. He wants international control.'

Japan's position loomed large, both in her claims to control the former German islands in the Pacific and her demand for reciprocity for Japanese citizens throughout the world. This latter 'equality clause', as it was called, was rejected out of hand by Hughes in agreement with the Australian cabinet. When the clause was voted down, Hughes cabled Watt that the Americans had tried to persuade the Japanese that the rejection was solely due to Australian intransigence ('a contemptible lie' was how his cable of 17 February described it), when in fact 11 of the delegates had voted against and the Americans had abstained. He later cabled with the other good news that Australia had been given a mandate over all ex-German islands and territories south of the equator except Nauru, with Samoa to become the responsibility of New Zealand. Moreover, the mandate was in the form Australia wished for, namely that she would have the power to make the same laws in mandated territories as pertained in the Commonwealth.

Hughes also reported on the matter of reparations to be paid by Germany to the Allies. And it was his position in this regard that brought contumely on his head from John Maynard Keynes, who attended the Peace Conference from January to June 1919 as principal Treasury representative, and had estimated that Germany's capacity to pay reparations was about £1000 million, a position completely at variance with Hughes' public demands that Germany be made to pay the full costs incurred by the Allies in the war. The committee set up by the imperial cabinet and chaired by Hughes found that Germany should pay £24 000 million. R.F. Harrod, in his biography of Keynes, wrote that Keynes held 'a passionate intellectual contempt for the trash of Hughes'. Keynes' view of his own Prime Minister, Lloyd George, was hardly more complimentary: 'How can I convey to the reader who does not know him any just impression of this extraordinary figure of our time, this syren, this goat-footed bard, this half-human visitor to our age from the hag ridden magic and enchanted woods of Celtic antiquity'. Effete, quintessentially English and Treasury-trained as Keynes was, it is hardly surprising that the raw energy and directness of Hughes and Lloyd George would have had that effect on him. Whatever the impact in terms of Germany's subsequent political development, in the event reparations remained largely unpaid and Australia got little of economic value from the deal, with around four-fifths of her war debt having to be paid by the Australian people.

The treaty was signed at 2 pm on 28 June 1919 in the great Hall of Mirrors at the Palace of Versailles, six months after the conference had begun and 48 years after the King of Prussia had been proclaimed German Emperor in the same room. The treaty redrew the map of Europe, established the right of small nations to govern themselves, and established the League of Nations as its guardian. Some years later Deane noted laconically that it was America who was the first to repudiate the treaty.

Chapter 9

Eclipsed but not extinguished

Initially greeted with acclaim and a degree of even adulation on his return, he was soon confronted with the myriad concerns of bread and butter politics. After the tumult of the war effort and two bruising conscription campaigns, the public at large quickly turned to the more mundane business of day-to-day living. Shortly after the return he turned his mind to some constitutional matters, particularly the vexed question of the appointment and role of the governor-general. A memorandum by him concerning the selection of governor-general demonstrated the disparate goads in his make-up: his respect for tradition and his capacity for original thought, his regard for the claims of the mother country, and his Australian nationalism. The memorandum spelled out the need for Australia to have a real and effective voice in the selection of the governor-general. Of course the final word would have to be with the King, but Australia should have the right of initiative and veto, and the list of possible candidates had to include Australians. Moreover, Australia should have the greater weight in making the eventual appointment.

The 21st of May 1921 saw Hughes embark again for England to attend another Imperial Conference. On this occasion the welcome was not as tumultuous as on his previous visit; the war was over and the times were out of joint for Hughes' portentous oratory. On 16 August, he attended a civic dinner in Bradford after having visited the Sheffield

Vickers Yard where he opined that the sooner countries went back to the gold standard the better. On the 17th he went to York, then on to Wales to Llansantffraid with Mary and to Caernarfon for the unveiling of Lloyd George's statue in Castle Square, staying again at the St George's Hotel, Llandudno, on the way. He visited France again, and again spoke in French, this time at Amiens.

Pushed out

Hughes returned to Australia on 28 September 1921 and noted that forces of disintegration were at work in his cabinet. In November he lost one of his foremost supporters when Cook went to become High Commissioner in London. The pre-sessional meeting of the National Party in June the following year saw Hughes depressed and in low spirits, with the deep fissures in the party more apparent than ever. In the aftermath of the war, problems abounded: a slump in the sugar industry, turmoil in the coalfields, loan concessions in London, repatriation. By August 1922, Hughes' ready optimism was again evident, but too much ground had been lost and his forced resignation came in February 1923 when Earle Page, the leader of the Country Party, having won the balance of power in the 1922 election, refused to serve in a coalition with Hughes as Prime Minister, preferring to join forces with Stanley Bruce, who had been Treasurer in Hughes' National Government.

The relations between Hughes and Bruce were proper but lukewarm. Bruce had not been party to destabilising the government and removing Hughes; rather he had been encouraged by Hughes to do the deal with Page. An exchange of letters between the two shows Bruce exhibiting a degree of angst over the position of Hughes' friend Pearce. Bruce wanted Pearce in the new administration but believed that he would not dream of doing anything that suggested the slightest degree of disloyalty to Hughes. Bruce asked Hughes to intervene and persuade his friend to accept a cabinet post, adding that he was perfectly aware what a 'big ask' that was. Hughes replied with a handwritten note: 'Will you come to my room, says the spider to the fly.' Hughes declined to intervene: that was a matter in his view strictly between Pearce and the new Prime Minister to be, Bruce. For Hughes, Bruce was 'a very conventional English Johnny'.

The *Herald* had written on 2 February 1923, just before Hughes' fall:

> In public life there have been men much sounder in judgement, richer in culture and infinitely less selfish and less vain but none so engaging in personality nor so variable in mood. At his worst Mr Hughes is perhaps the rudest, most uncouth, most morose personality that has stalked large upon the Australian stage. At his best, the richest in humour, the most brilliant and engaging in conversation, the most appealing in personality. He is the most incongruous man we have known.

After his fall, the *Australian National Review* wrote on 19 February 1923: 'The mightier man, the mightier is the thing that makes him honoured or begets him hate, For greatest scandal waits on greatest state'. The Sydney *Telegraph* wrote that Hughes had been 'eclipsed but not extinguished'. Other newspapers referred to the event and Hughes in rather different terms, one describing him as, 'little more than an animated brain, a little wizened giant'.

The manner of his ousting remained no doubt a sore point and there was ample speculation that his return to high office was only a matter of time which Hughes' attitude and demeanour did nothing to gainsay. However, there is hardly any trace of him indulging in nostalgia or crying over spilt milk: his was a Heracleitan view of life, all was flux, you could never throw a stone into the same river twice: 'The joy of life is not in attaining but in striving, achievement has a tendency to turn into Dead Sea fruit.'

In an interesting aside, in December 1923 Hughes broke his ankle by stepping into a garage well and had to spend Christmas in bed. This is somewhat bizarre — an exact repetition of what he said had befallen him on his first day arriving in Brisbane years earlier; it is perhaps a typical example of his embellishment of his arrival in Australia, using an incident which really did occur but much later on.

Billy Hughes

A 'diabolical hypocrite'

His low spirits in these years would have been exacerbated by a long-running, ugly and blistering dispute with his elder daughter Ethel over his lack of provision for the daughters from his relationship with Elizabeth Cutts, and it is perhaps surprising that the exceedingly bitter letters from her to Hughes were not expunged from his files, for they do little for his reputation:

> Mr Mulligan [the solicitor] told me that you had been in to see him and that you were not going to stand for blackmail. It is not exactly that. You know very well that such steps as I will be forced to take are your own doing. We cannot appeal to your love. Too late is all. And your conduct has been deplorable. You blame us for your life and our part in it. What would Mr Mulligan or any person think if they knew the miserable truth. You should be on your knees asking our pardon and trying to atone for everything. Instead you have been cruel in every way. In fact you would be very pleased if we all passed out. You tell Mr Mulligan that if I am not careful you will cut me out of your will. That sort of talk is silly and empty, as you have not the slightest intention of leaving any one of us a brass farthing. Besides you will live on for ever. So threats of this kind would never alarm me.
>
> The whole thing is this that you must fix our incomes so that you cannot withdraw them at your pleasure. And £3 a week is very small for us. Dolly cannot possibly live on £2 and you know it. Also Dolly and I want a trip so she can meet decent people and a chance to marry well if she desires it. If poor Dolly really knew the truth about things she would shoot you and then herself. Dolly and I will see you before [we] arrange a meeting with Mr Mulligan. It must be before you go away. Please do not try bullying me, as I will not stand for it. My nerves are bad and I cannot afford to be upset. My life has been one long fight against the odds. I do not want to expose you. This is for you to decide. Why should you be allowed to go on as if you were everything to be desired in a man, the emblem of goodness, father etc...

The date of the letter is unclear but was sometime in 1922, when she gave her address as 1 Eurowa Flats, 139 Ocean Beach. Following the letter there must have been further consultations involving Mr Mulligan, for there is a reference in later correspondence to an agreement of 18 December 1922 between the children and Hughes.

The dispute was obviously of long standing, and one can only speculate on its origins and the degree of acerbity in Ethel's resentment and denouncement of her father. Partly it must have been due to the father's second marriage, Ethel's loss of the role of looking after her father, the burdens of taking care of the children and bad feeling between her and Dame Mary. A letter from Mary to Hughes recorded the problems she had encountered with the children who had been staying with her:

> When your letter came I wept tears of joy. Before it arrived I felt frigid and alone ... The boys never gave me any message from you at all except the letter, not a word about their clothes etc. I knew they wanted shirts — and I got them two each so they have gone back now. I was anxious about their clothes and wanted to send them others. Even if they do not care for me — they were both sullen — and never spoke a half dozen words to me and I practically knew nothing of what they needed or what they had. I gave the girls five shillings each to go on with, not knowing what arrangements you had made. I did not give the boys anything. They were not justified in acting as they did, and I feel it was actuated by others. In any case Esther ought to be the first person to teach them their duty — as children. I don't admire their behaviour at all and she does not seem sincere. I would not stoop to quarrel with her but never want to see her again. I want to pay Mrs Brown for the board this month, if you have not paid it. What will the exact amount be? They went on Monday afternoon late — in time for dinner and left on the Sunday 11th February. They were there three weeks all but a day and three quarters — don't smile at my way of putting the subject — but it is the best an untrained brain can do to make the matter clear to you. I asked Mrs Brown to send her bill — she has not done so yet — the girls left and said it was six pounds. I asked her to ask Mrs Brown to post the bill to me. I don't think one ought to pay for a whole day at least they were not there.

Ethel, far more than Mary, was clearly strongly affected by her father's stinginess; the ethos, social mores and conditions of the times were such that young ladies of a particular background or upbringing generally did not work, and, despite Australia's comparative lack of pretension and class divisions, this was still a distinctly colonial period with powerful sentiments of what was and was not regarded as proper in polite society, let alone in respect of daughters of a prime minister. In short, fathers were expected to take care of single daughters. However, the evidence strongly implies that Ethel's manifest spleen was even more predicated on the fact that the children had no rights under the law of that time because they were illegitimate.

The dispute with her father continued in subsequent years. A letter from Ethel dated 20 March 1925, concerning the arrangements Hughes had made for the girls, revealed her anxiety. She states: 'Mr Mulligan who drew it up knows nothing about our family circumstances and I am told that it is no good unless I can get an opinion from somebody who does know all the circumstances.' She referred to having written previously at Christmas 'without a reply', adding 'if you had any natural feelings for us you must have answered ... I can hardly understand your apparent lack of knowledge relating to children in our circumstances. Yet you are a barrister at law. I do not wish to have any further dealings with your lawyer Mr Mulligan.'

By June of the same year a lawyer, A. Holman, wrote from his chambers in Phillip Street, Sydney; he referred to a document Mulligan had shown him and opined that it is 'a fair and indeed, liberal arrangement' but not enforceable because of the 'privacy essential' which 'makes registration impossible', and recommended drawing up a further document to take account of the December 1922 agreement. What Ethel wanted was some kind of copper-bottomed guarantee which her father could not alter.

In a long letter to her father dated 31 May 1925, Ethel agreed to the regular payments as set out but maintained the amount to be left them on his demise was illegal. She had been advised by a friend, she said, 'that children like us are placed outside the pale of the law's protection' and continued, in a tone similar to many of her letters:

> do you realise what you have done against us. And yet you dare to act as if we were not fit to claim you as a father. How you can be content to live as you do knowing in your heart all the misery you have brought us, without in any way ever showing us the least regret on your part, you should feel very proud of yourself... Now read this very carefully. I have definitely made up my mind that this sort of thing must alter or I will take some desperate measures to make you feel your true position. I am your daughter and this being so I inherit your fighting capabilities and nothing will deter me from doing what I consider my duty... However the fact remains that we are your children and must be treated as such, in as far as money is concerned, as you can do nothing else for us now. The few paltry pounds that we dragged out of you on the eve of the last election, does not amount to more than £400 per year — a princely sum for a man of your wealth to give three daughters of whom he has robbed of their birthright.
>
> You and your present family can afford to live in luxury, motor car etc, live like a man of refinement, go to church affairs even preach in the church, you talk so much about, you diabolical hypocrite, you should worry for the heavens to fall and crush you in your dreadful blasphemy. What would all those people think if they knew you as you really are, a black hearted villain that brings five unfortunate children into the world and then kicks them to hell at the first opportunity, a truly noble man. And you can feel proud and happy at the way you carried out our dead mother's trust in you... I will go to the wealthiest and most influential paper man in Australia and tell him the story right from the start... We are your daughters although illegal, but this is not our fault and we refuse to be penalised for your actions. If you refuse I swear everybody will know the ghastly double life of the Hon. WM Hughes... I also intend appealing to Parliament to help me. There was some talk of passing an act to legalise children in our position... Why should we suffer and at your death your wife and child get everything...

Ethel said she would not be unreasonable, and that an agreement could be drawn up through a Mr D. Hall. She proceeded to ask for an increase in the monthly allowance for her sisters to £16 per month and to £32 for herself. In addition she wanted a reasonable percentage of his wealth on his demise, 'not the paltry sixteen or eighteen hundred set down in the present valueless agreement'. The final words of the letter were equally frank: 'I do not trust you in any shape or form ... My threats are not idle. Ethel Hughes.'

In August of 1925, Ethel referred to Mr Hall having seen Hughes regarding the settlement, and Hughes' agreement to change the last part (presumably the clauses regarding the will). She had to leave matters as they were, she said, since her divorce was going through and she was tired of writing to him. She added that, if he could not do any better by her and her sisters with a more generous settlement, she would go to see Jack Lang, the Premier of New South Wales, and lay the whole case before him and get him to have a bill passed 'legitimising children in our position'. The situation was one of 'infamy', Lily 'always sick' and Dolly 'little better'. She gave him three weeks to 'think it over'. With a general election imminent one can imagine that the threat of exposure and possible scandal was in her mind and would have had a degree of resonance with Hughes as well.

By November Ethel seemed to have won the day, since there is on record a draft agreement dated 1925 (though with no month or day given) between William Morris Hughes and 'Ethel Mary Bourke of Manly/Married woman, Dorothea Hughes of Manly Spinster, Lily Hughes of Wellington New Zealand Spinster'. It refers to the earlier agreement of 18 December 1922 and stipulates that £5000 will be invested and the proceeds given to his daughters on his death. However, a year later barrister and solicitor Joan Rosanove wrote to Hughes on 18 February 1926 making representations on behalf of his daughters, arguing that the present arrangements in their regard were unsatisfactory and asking for a more definite arrangement.

A letter from Ethel's daughter sent to him sometime in 1927 said that her mother had nearly been killed when the Manly Ferry rammed the little skiff she was sailing in. Whether mollified by an eventual financial settlement, or chastened by intimations of mortality after her accident, Ethel had enclosed with her daughter's letter one of her own, dated 2 September 1927, showing a markedly altered tone from her earlier letters:

> My dear Father ... I am very, very regretful that you are so estranged from us all. I do not expect that you will ever forget or forgive me. What I did I had to do ... Anyhow leave me out, hate me as you wish and probably do. But do forgive the others. Dolly is a very sweet and clever girl. She has never hurt you by word or deed and Billy, he has his darling little babies that surely must give you very great pleasure to see them occasionally. Do you know that Lily has been very ill for the last year or so and Charley has been wonderful to her. If it upsets your present domestic life you can be discreet. I fully appreciate the fact that you must not disturb the serenity of your present home.
>
> If Billy had not told me that once you expressed regret that we were all so disunited I would not have written this letter. As for me please do not let your hatred of me prejudice you against my brothers and sisters. You told Bill I was a very bad woman. Well perhaps I am from the angle you view the situation. We all think we are right so it is futile to argue. My battles started very early in life. Mother died when I was fourteen. You were very difficult and hard. I fully appreciate the fact that you are an exceptionally clever and brilliant man and that the affairs of the world have always kept you busy ... Well my dear father I will stop now. There are many things I would like to say but I feel it is futile and you would not understand how I feel, your daughter Ethel'.

There are no further references to Ethel in Hughes' papers except for a mention in his last will, which suggests that some form of reconciliation had transpired. Farmer Whyte, writing in 1957, recorded her as having lived in California for more than 20 years and having a daughter, Betty, who had become well known as a portrait painter and had won a Stacey Award, a prestigious grant for painters.

From the material on record, Ethel emerges as easily the most 'feisty' of his children and more the chip off the Hughes block than her father would have wished for. The estrangement between them, however, did not extend to his other children. They sent him cards regularly on his birthday and for Christmas; a typical one from Dolly reads: 'Dear Dad, I hope you have a good Xmas dinner despite the shortage of women cooks and good health and happiness from your affectionate daughter Dolly.' Hughes in turn was constant in remembering their birthdays, often forwarding presents — a practice he continued with grandchildren and nieces and nephews in later years. The extant correspondence between him and his children, including Arthur, frequently concerns money — he made regular disbursements to Dolly and Lily right up to his death — but also indicates a warm relationship and respect even if, to a large extent, Hughes kept them at a certain physical distance.

Notwithstanding his problems both political and familial, he bought a piece of land at Sassafras at a cost of £250 for an orchard and £50 per acre for the Ty Coed estate. Frank Green, a long-serving clerk of the House of Representatives, wrote in the *Sun Herald* of 3 May 1959 that the place was looked after by: a one-eyed attendant, a returned soldier known as Cyclops; a personal bodyguard, a Salvation Army captain named Jenkins reputed to have been a prize fighter; and a house keeper, Mrs Lloyd, whose husband was supposed to look after the garden. Mr Lloyd would write periodically to relate items of Sassafras news, such as the death of his wife, but also to ask for payment of wages, which were in most cases paid four or five months in arrears. Hughes enjoyed riding and took a constitutional daily ride when at Sassafras usually on his favourite horse, called Darkie. In early June 1922 he was again thrown from his horse and again broke a collarbone. Darkie went on to a ripe old age, dying in February 1938. In March 1922 he protested vigorously to the president of the Shire Council of Fern Tree Gully against a proposal to build a slaughterhouse opposite Ty Coed; the Fern Tree Gully area subsequently became one of the first designated national parks of Australia.

He kept detailed accounts of all domestic expenditure and expected Mary to do likewise: 'April 11–July 3 Massage treatment £24.0 Bought cigarettes, brilliantine, toilet vinegar.' He also maintained regular records of his financial situation and his stocks and shares: '1923 17 Jan. Statement from Commercial Bank Melbourne — debit £950.8.8. Stock held £30,000. Sydney-overdrawn £438; £5000 deposit, 20 debentures of £100 each.' Frequently the children's names are written in Hughes' distinctive shorthand, although the addresses are in normal script. The use of shorthand was clearly to disguise from Mary both the extent of his continuing relationship with his first family as well as the regular monies he forwarded to his children.

In their early years, Hughes' financial records, including bank statements, receipts and cheque stubs, reveal normal expenditure on the children: £1 a month to Ethel when the children lived in Gore Hill, £5 for Dolly's operation, £2 for Dolly's cloak, money for dresses, gloves and coats, fares for the children from Sydney to Melbourne, a trip to Hobart. There are receipts from the Church of England Grammar School for payment of fees for Lily and Ethel, £8 per month to a Dr Stowell to cover Charles' attendance at a clinic, and monthly payments to cover Bill's attendance at the Hawkesbury College and travelling expenses.

At the same time, and again in seeming contradiction to his overweaning prudence with money, a letter came from Mabel, his stepson Arthur's wife, to thank him profusely for his generosity: 'Many, many thanks for the cheque, you are very, very good to us but then you have always been so.'

A pensive young Billy (*centre row, fourth from left*) at Llandudno Grammar School, c.1870. When he was seven his mother died, and he was sent to live with his Aunt Mary in this Welsh seaside town.

Bryn Rosa, on Abbey Road in Llandudno, where Hughes lived with his Aunt Mary.

Hughes (*front right*) with members of the Labour Party (later spelled 'Labor') in the first Federal Parliament in 1901.

Members of the Trolly, Draymen and Carters Union in 1905, with Hughes as President (*seated centre front*). Apart from the school of hard knocks, his political education was fostered in the early trade union movement.

(LEFT) A portrait from 1908. Unlike the many later photographs emphasising his crabby features, here we have an image of rather a striking, even handsome, man.

(RIGHT) This 1912 cartoon was entitled 'A Hard Case for Labor' — a reference to Hughes' series of policy tracts called 'The Case for Labor'. Readers would have chuckled at the insinuation that he was more than a handful even for his own compadres.

(LEFT) Hughes being carried along George Street in 1919. Despite splitting the country over conscription, he was given a hero's welcome on return from the Paris Peace Conference.

Hughes and some of his family in 1919: wife Mary, daughter Helen, son Bill and pugnacious companion. Certainly in his own estimation Hughes belonged to the bulldog breed.

Portrait of Dame Mary Hughes, c.1905. Mary was a notable figure in her own right, receiving an OBE for services during World War I, and remaining a strong advocate for women's rights.

Canberra in the 1920s. Although initially favouring a New South Wales site, Hughes was soon won around to the suitability of Canberra as the new capital.

Known as the terror of the Sydney-Canberra highway, Hughes had a love affair with cars all his long life. He acquired his last licence at 89, a year before he died.

Hughes' daughter Helen aged seven — his 'gleam of eternal sunshine'.

Hughes at a cricket match with 21-year-old Helen in 1936. His heart broke when, but a year after this photograph was taken, she died in London giving birth to a son.

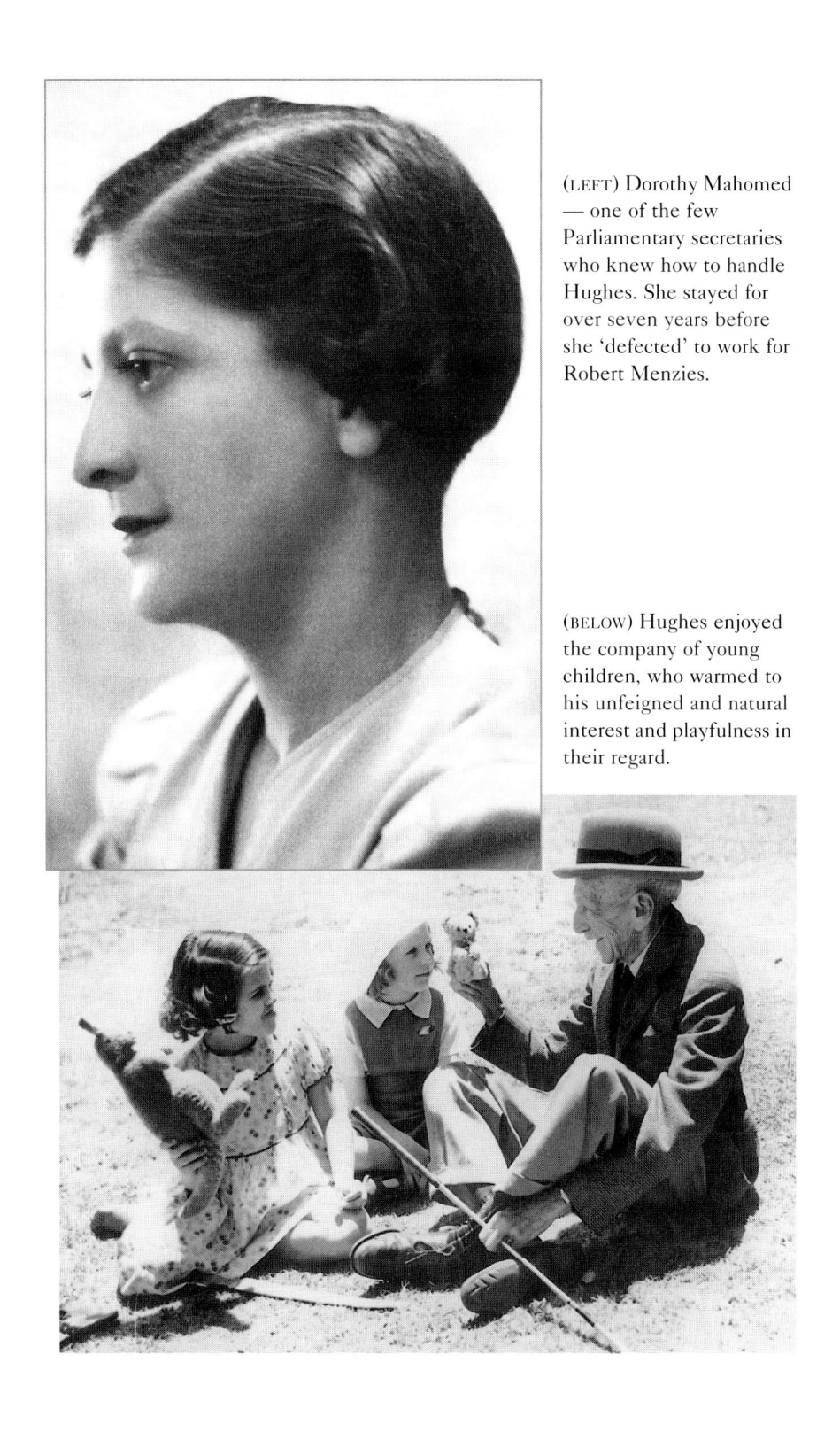

(LEFT) Dorothy Mahomed — one of the few Parliamentary secretaries who knew how to handle Hughes. She stayed for over seven years before she 'defected' to work for Robert Menzies.

(BELOW) Hughes enjoyed the company of young children, who warmed to his unfeigned and natural interest and playfulness in their regard.

On his favourite horse, Darkie, at the family property at Sassafras. Despite complaining about the costs of running the property, he enjoyed his time spent there and would ride daily.

Hughes' 90th birthday in 1952 — a mutual admiration society with Dame Enid Lyons. He was able to crack a joke a bare few weeks before his death.

Chapter 10

The frustrating years

Without the cares of high office, Hughes and Dame Mary now had time to look for a residence, and although Parliament was still in Melbourne they bought a house in Nelson Rd, Lindfield, Sydney, in November 1924. By then Sydney had grown into one of the major trading cities in the world, with a population of over a million — a rapid development from the 53 000 of 1853 and the 400 000 of 1890. The usual rivalry between Australia's two largest cities had been exacerbated over the issue of choosing the national capital, and there were fascinating claims and counterclaims in the press vaunting the perceived pre-eminence of the one over the other — 'marvellous Melbourne' on one hand and 'scintillating Sydney' on the other. For Sir Robert Garran, Sydney at the time was, 'a careless beauty who has neglected her appearance whilst Melbourne has made up for her comparative lack of natural advantages by careful grooming'. A very different opinion was expressed by one McKnight of the Crown Solicitor's Office — at least in respect of Sydney — who wrote of the squalid streets of the inner suburbs and ruffians who 'lived like Nature's bastards not her sons'. But of course he may have been a Melbournian.

Although Hughes looked forward to moving into the new house, he expostulated, 'but I would like something to do'. There is evidence that Hughes would have been happy to accept the appointment as High Commissioner in London in the period after his exit from office but that Bruce would have none of it. Mary wrote to her husband in March 1926 that it seemed strange and unjust to her that the position was going to a Dr Howse: 'Bruce must certainly bear you great personal animosity.

I would be glad if you got it. Australia has not been sufficiently grateful to you for all you have done. And it would be nice to get away.' The Melbourne *Herald* strongly supported the possibility of Hughes going to London, noting in particular the extent of contacts and friendships Hughes had forged in Britain during his visits as Prime Minister.

Hughes had considered selling the Sassafras property, Ty Coed, and had written to his son Charles to alert him that it might have to go under the auctioneer's hammer since Parliament would soon be moving away from Melbourne to Canberra. 'Besides it costs too much', he added. 'The horses are eating their heads off. I never ride them and keep Lloyd mainly to grow feed for them, which he doesn't do very well.' He acknowledged, however, that Helen was much happier there than at Lindfield. Mary wrote from Sassafras, where she was preparing the house for sale, 'Please do not worry about politics … there is so much treachery and deceit.' She added that she had fixed various things around the house 'but it won't come to much and no-one could have done it for less'.

In the same period she commented, in a letter to a friend, on the perception of her husband by some: 'Spending himself in public service is something quite beyond most people's understanding. It's rather terrifying to a wife … And then he is always in the highest spirits when driving himself to the utmost capacity … when I read some of the things said about my husband I simply fail to recognise him — they picture someone who is a complete stranger to me. His motives, according to his opponents are ascribed to things that have never occurred to him.'

Ty Coed and its seven acres of land was put up for sale in August 1928 and an offer of £2000 was made in September but turned down since Hughes, exhibiting his usual canniness, wanted £2500. It was not offered for sale again until February 1941.

'The meeting place'

The move to establish Parliament in Canberra had made progress when Hughes set up an advisory committee under Sir John Sulman to spur the start of building. An anthem composed by his co-parliamentarians had been presented to him on his return from the Peace Conference:

> Billy, Billy, Billy my boy
> What are you waiting for now
> You promised us Canberra some time last June
> And so did your Ministers Poynton and Groom
> All the members keep on asking us
> Which day what day
> We will get from Vic away
> Billy, Billy, Billy my boy
> What are you waiting for now?

The commitment to creating a new capital city had been made in the Constitution in 1901, and preliminary steps to find a suitable site had been started by the New South Wales Parliament as early as 1899. In 1902, a pilgrimage was made by a select committee of MPs to inspect some 40 proposed sites, with Hughes joining the group charged with examining those in New South Wales. Eventually six possible sites were chosen, of which the main choices were Albury, Dalgety and Yass-Canberra. Albury lost out when the parliamentary committee set up to report on the sites arrived in the town and found it experiencing its worst dust storm ever. Dalgety was placed first and the decision affirmed by the Federal Parliament — a demented decision according to Hughes since it was in his view one of the coldest spots in Australia. The New South Wales Government, however, refused to give its assent and the issue remained in abeyance for some years.

The matter was reopened in 1906 and Yass-Canberra chosen by the Federal Parliament as the preferred location. Although Dalgety tried a rearguard action to have its claims re-examined, as of 1911 the matter was settled. Hughes would have preferred Sydney but became reconciled to the choice of Canberra, was present at the laying of the foundation stone in March 1913, visited the site from time to time, and took a real interest in its development. In 1927 the Parliament moved from Melbourne to its new home in the traditional lands of the Ngunnawal people, Canberra, 'the meeting place', although at one stage it looked as if the capital might be called 'Anzac'. Hughes was one of the first to buy a block of land in what later became 28 Mugga Way and is now a Carmelite monastery: a plaque to this effect was erected at the entrance porch. One of the oldest houses in Canberra was number 24 Mugga Way, Calthorpe House, home of the Calthorpe family, where Hughes would be a regular visitor for a 'spot' — in other words, a whisky. He owned the lease of No. 28 from September 1925 until March 1936 but never built on the site, his and Dame Mary's preferred place of residence during parliamentary sessions was the Canberra Hotel, where full board was £1 10s.

Getting away from Canberra when he could, Hughes took up doing odd jobs around the new house in Lindfield, began carpentry and joined Leichhardt Rowing Club. He played golf and was a member of the Victoria Golf Club and the Killara Golf Club; he once recorded getting a 44 for the first nine holes in February 1931 but admitted that he was not in the first flight of golfers. Various sources suggest he was a bit of a hacker, known for making up his own rules as he thrashed his way around the various courses. Often he would hold up the field with a prolonged search for his ball in the rough and fail to wave through following players. Bachli, his masseur, who normally accompanied him, always bought the same kind of ball and all the same number: after a minute or two of his boss's futile looking, he would drop another ball with a 'Here it is' and Hughes would be content. The chairman of his first election meeting was a Percy Hunter, who remained a friend over the years and was esteemed by Hughes, who was to marvel that Hunter still played golf at 90 years of age at the Elenora club. Hughes was also made an honorary member of Wentworth Golf Club during his time in England in 1932. C.S. Daley wrote of Hughes' friendship with Sir Robert Garran and that they frequently played golf together, the rounds punctuated by caustic but often witty comments. When Hughes played at Canberra Royal Golf Club in the springtime, a policeman often accompanied him to keep the magpies away from his long ears. He also enjoyed cricket and, according to the *Evening News*, at 68 he could wield a 'pretty bat'.

Daley also recalled a parliamentary occasion when a member asked the Minister for Trade whether an embargo had been placed on the export of polo ponies to India; quick as a flash Hughes shot to his feet: 'the answer is "neigh".' Daley, who knew Hughes for some 45 years, was quoted in the *Canberra Times* as saying that Hughes was 'unpredictable, difficult to live with and to work for, resourceful, a savage opponent, some would say even unscrupulous, yet displaying on occasions many unsuspected facets of dignity, real humanity and humour'. Writing in October 1949 for the *Herald*, Bachli also reminisced about his years with Hughes, how he used to massage him twice a day on occasions, that his boss was largely a vegetarian, eating little, weighing just eight stone, and that he did not often bet, 'But at 85 he can kick a hat out of a man's hand held shoulder height'.

In 1924 Hughes was issued with his first driving licence[1] and acquired his first car. During his trip to America, accompanied by Mary and the young Helen, who was left in California with a governess, he bought a new car (a Flint) and had it shipped back to Australia, for which he had to pay £105 duty. The car was unique in Australia, being the first in the country to have balloon tyres, but was sadly destroyed in a fire at Sam Wright's coach building works in 1927. Hughes exchanged it for another Flint but transferred his allegiance to a Buick in 1935 and frequently, being of a litigious nature, exchanged letters with the Buick distributors in Australia as well as with the NRMA. His driving licence of 1940 described him as being 5ft 7ins tall (a seeming gain of 2 inches in 20 years!), eyes blue, hair brown, complexion fair. He loved driving and maintained an avid interest in cars all his life and sold his last car, still a Buick, in 1951 for £650.

The *Herald* wrote that for 25 years he was the terror of the Sydney-Canberra road and held the record for the 200-mile run for many years when it was but a string of potholes, adding that few would travel with him. One of his drivers said, 'When you are driving you can't go fast enough for the old cow, and when he's driving the car can't go fast enough.' Dame Mary must have been blessed with a remarkable degree of sangfroid, since her preference was for gentle perambulation; as

Hughes put it: 'What Dame Mary calls moving is to my way of thinking a kind of exaggerated standing still'. Most reports of his driving noted his recklessness, appetite for high speed and frequent accidents. Leo Amery wrote, regarding one of his accidents, 'I see you have been trying to see how many eucalyptus trees you can knock down in a motor car'. On 7 February 1951, at the age of 89, he was granted a renewed driving licence after passing a medical examination. His driver for several years, R.J. Tracey, commenting on his boss, said, 'he liked driving fast, cards [his favourite game was '500'] and billiards: A man of swift changes, a remarkable Australian despite his moods and tantrums.' After leaving Hughes' employ he asked his old boss for a loan of £150 pounds to buy himself into a garage business. Hughes also enjoyed horseriding and as early as 1900 there was an account of him on horseback in Sydney with 40 or so shearers in a trade union display as part of the Commonwealth celebrations.

The year 1924 also saw him taking an interest in the building of the Sydney Harbour Bridge, brought to his attention by the English Electric Company of Australia Ltd. He enjoyed the Melbourne Cup and took great delight in having backed the winner, Backwood. In November he commented on the UK elections: 'The Liberals are out for good — they were little Englanders, mumblers of a shrivelled shibboleth. I'm sorry for Asquith as a man but as a political leader he was hopeless. What is my distinguished countryman L.G. going to do?'

Health matters: Mens sana in corpore sano?

Most who have written about Billy Hughes have referred to his continuing bouts of bad health, some arguing that he was a hypochondriac. We know that his doctor during the Melbourne years was Marmaduke Rose of Burlington Chambers, 92 Collins St, but there are no medical records in Hughes' papers for the period he lived there nor for the years he lived in Sydney. The most exhaustive account of his medical condition was provided during his visit on a lecture tour to the US in 1924. While in New York in June he went to see a Dr Charles Jack Hunt for a consultation. The report of the good doctor was comprehensive: he was not to eat certain kinds of food unless he did more exercise, and his ability to digest and chemically use was improved by artificial methods (drug therapy etc). It was very important: that he avoided nervous fatigue, engage in daily exercise, have a balanced diet with reduced amount of foods of animal origin, increase his fluid intake. He was to have regular rest periods and follow a prescribed diet, intestinal elimination should not be brought about by the constant use of laxative drugs by mouth — high colon irrigations once weekly being the best method. Were this to be impossible then he was to take enemas. The doctor added: 'I believe your depression ... is of physio-chemical origin.'

This diagnosis followed a thorough set of examinations carried out between 4 and 17 June. The doctor's more detailed conclusions were as follows:

Chief complaints:
- Recurrent periods of depression alternating with euphoria
- Progressive loss of hearing
- Dyspepsia lasting many years

...

Duodenum showed a constant and marked irregularity in the first position, which was demonstrable in all positions. There was a definite temporary but pathological duodenal stasis in the lower portion of the descending limb ... considerable degree of colon stasis ... moderate degree of arthritis involving the 5th lumbar vertebrae and the lumbo-sacral articulation.

Diagnoses:
- Duodenal ulcer with periduodenal adhesions
- Colon stasis associated with chronic passive congestion of the cecum and appendix
- Chronic arthritis (spinal)
- Chronic perineuritis
- Cholesterinaemia and mild nitrogen retention.

Throughout his long life he exhibited only a tiny appetite. When he was chairman and secretary of the Waterside Workers Federation and Labour MP for West Sydney, he had a very limited diet (a young lad named C.R. Hall's main job was popping out to get peanuts for him — 'that was about the only thing he lived on'). He had a profound disinterest in food and found formal dinners and lunches a trial, but retained a lifelong liking for baked apple, and, suffering from chronic dyspepsia, he was constantly chewing pills for the condition. This would not have been surprising in a man of stronger digestive capacity confronted with the often gargantuan meals served at the time. An old digger wrote to him reminding him of one of his visits to the front, to a little village called Hume St Hume, to a unit commanded by Lieutenant General Sir Talbot Hobbs. A dinner was served in his honour at the Australian Corps GOC Mess on 12 April 1919, the menu consisting of ten separate dishes, from 'potage a la Julienne' to 'Gateau St Georges'. Dinners in Australia at the time were no less sumptuous, the menu for an official dinner he attended in Melbourne on 4 September 1919 consisting again of ten dishes, including 'turtle soup' and 'roast turkey en truffes'.

There were frequent references to him picking at his food, and prolonged mastication. In an undated letter Dame Mary wrote:

> Meals have always been something to forget about, — the proverbial woman's 'something on a tray' is also true in his case and either Helen or I have to stand over him to make him eat that, — it's usually a little fruit. But his energy seems inexhaustible. He is always dashing off to meetings and it's often 2 or 3, sometimes 4 in the morning before he gets home ... He says he can't spare the time to be ill ...

However, there are many letters on file regretting his inability to attend various functions and events due to ill health. He took either hexamine tablets plain or with methylene blue for pyelitis. There is also a reference to him trying Sanatogen on one occasion but no indication whether it did 'fortify the over forties'. In a letter of 7 March 1922 about his vaccines he wrote that 'enteritictis' was very difficult to get rid of and that massage was very beneficial. He once avowed to being a wretched sleeper at the best of times.

In one letter he displayed a stoic and humorous attitude to his agues. Sir Arthur Streeton, the artist, had written to him: 'I suppose the silkworm enjoys nibbling away at his mulberry leaves. The artist is much the same, his best works created in solitude: like the silkworm and later on the critics and dealers quarrel over the lengths of silk.' Hughes replied:

> Dear Sir Arthur,
> Your letter and the illuminating sketch of the artist blacklegging on the Bricklayers Union (Penalty 1,00000000, or Death or Both) to hand. I hope you are now at once penitent and well. But if not penitent at least well. I've had an experience, which but for the knight-errantry with the trowel is a palimpsest of yours. I got much better, amazingly and resplendently better — in other and more prosaic words — quite well — And then a relapse in which, though I am still floundering — feeling miserable and wondering in a feeble sort of way why I ever took the trouble to be born.
>
> And this my dear Sir Arthur is the state of man, Today he puts forth the tender leaves of hope, to-morrow blossoms and bears his blushing honours thick upon him, the third day comes the flu, the rotten, thrice-accursed flu — and nips his root and then he falls as we do. But no more of these sickly meanderings, it is enough that so far we have contrived to keep out of the cemetery. With me I confess this is not merely a passing whim but a burning fanatical passion. And doubtless with you too ...

There is also one letter on file from Dame Mary to Sir Arthur reporting that a trip to Katoomba had done her husband the world of good but that she had found the Blue Mountains inexpressibly irritating (though the letter is devoid of any explanation why they should have had that effect on her).

Hughes was equally expansive writing to his dentist, having lost a bit of his dentures: 'I sank into the arms of Morpheus (not Patricia Murphy). I placed my teeth under my pillow ... In the morning they were gone! The only gold part — gone. Perhaps I've swallowed it. I am coming to see you!'

While Minister of Health, Hughes penned an article for the *Telegraph* expounding his own views regarding 'good living'. The basic cause of ill health in the modern world was, he maintained, 'a devitalised and unbalanced dietary regime' and urged 'moderation in everything'. Hughes enjoyed a glass of whisky but was not much of a drinker; however, he was a regular smoker, and many photographs show him either with a cigarette dangling from one side of his mouth or held almost theatrically between his long bony fingers. He became interested at one point in the possibility of making and marketing cigarettes from eucalyptus leaves which were to be called 'Euco'.

The Acousticon

Most writers and commentators have referred to his progressive deafness but there is also clear evidence that, just as with Winston Churchill, he used it as an effective tool — such as during speeches at the Peace Conference in debate with Wilson — and that on occasions he was not as deaf as people thought: he once said to a journalist that a man was a fool who failed to take advantage of his defects. On 4 June 1908 he bought, for £5/15s/6d, an Acousticon, a very large hearing aid by today's standards, which accompanied him thereafter in different versions. It had a central box and two leads for the very large ear pieces and a lead to the electricity point. On one occasion in September 1925 a certain John Hume had the misfortune of running over Hughes' Acousticon in his car; Hughes pursued the matter with vigour, making a formal claim against Mr Hume for damages.

Through the years there were many references to his hearing problems. He wrote to a Dr Vincent Nesfield, of Harley Street, London, describing his condition as catarrhal deafness and seeking advice on a suggestion that he should have an aurist scrape away the granulations at the mouth of the Eustachian tubes. He wrote frequently to the Acousticon manufacturers and became very annoyed when the government imposed a 22 per cent customs duty on American hearing aids. Many people wrote to him asking for advice on their hearing problems and he never failed to reply. And one wonders to what extent his own medical concerns contributed to his continuing interest in handicapped people and their problems. His letters also showed more than the normal sympathy for the ailments and illnesses of his friends and colleagues.

He was greatly impressed, for example, by the story of a fellow Welshman, Owain ap Llwyd (known as Owen Lloyd in Australia), who had been rendered nearly blind by a mining accident at Gundagai yet recovered to make a worthwhile life for himself. Hughes wrote to him: 'Your life has been an interesting one and like my own represents a triumph over difficulties. Perhaps it is a characteristic of Welsh people to ignore difficulties.'[2]

There can be little doubt that, apart from the rigours of his upbringing and early trials in the land of his adoption, both Hughes' deafness and chronic dyspepsia contributed hugely to observers' view of him as peppery, short-tempered and belligerent. And yet there is other testimony of his capacity to charm and delight, even on occasion his enemies: Jack Lang, one time premier of New South Wales and no great fan of Hughes, commented on an ABC program on Hughes,[3] that he could 'get on with most people when he put his mind to it'.

Chapter 11
Familial concerns

Out of office Hughes had more time to reflect on his relationship with his children, who were now in their twenties and shaping their own futures. His stepson Arthur enrolled in Strolls Business College in Sydney and graduated with a qualification as an accountant. The first reference to him in Hughes' papers was his involvement in the Bellinger affair, the second in a letter from Arthur telling him not to worry about his health but to be more concerned about his own and also seeking Hughes' help regarding a possible job at Army Headquarters at Duntroon in Canberra. Wendy Hughes, the actress, in a conversation with Diana Williams (Hughes' great-granddaughter), said that she believed she was descended from the Elizabeth Cutts side of the family and confirmed that Arthur was Hughes' stepson.

Requests for support in getting a job came to Hughes from his other two sons as well, following their return from the war to Australia. Throughout the 1920s a wealth of letters cover Bill's time as a qualified dairy supervisor living in lodgings in St Kilda, Melbourne, acquiring a wife, Hersee, and fathering two children, Beryl May and William Morris. Hughes was active in promoting his son's interests, often putting down the required earnest for different tenders Bill had bid for. On one such occasion Hughes approached a senior civil servant in Canberra, Sir John Baltes, in regard to his son: 'he's a hard case, went to war with Charlie, a younger but much steadier edition of the same immortal publication', adding that his son had won the Military Medal, collected some wounds, come home and cared for cows for a season. Was there any chance of getting him a job? 'He could superintend road work, curbing and guttering or any work of that class. He is willing to come to Canberra.'

A letter the following year showed that Bill and his family had moved to Canberra and were living in Jardine Street, Kingston. Bill asked his father for help again, to enable him to make a deposit applying for a concreting franchise. In July he sent a cheque to liquidate his debt to his father, reported that the job was turning out quite well and proffered many thanks for his father's help, adding: 'the baby is as black as pots and hard to recognise apart from his ginger hair'. Just over a week later, however, he wrote to say that he had been 'put off', but had been offered a position as a labourer, a job he had never done before. He liked Canberra and wanted to stay. He did not think that Sir John could have helped. Over more than a year thereafter there was an exchange of letters on the tendering process, with Hughes being consistently helpful and industrious on Bill's behalf.

Other than in his letters to Helen, Hughes was at his most paternal in his relationship with his youngest son, Charles, with whom he maintained a regular exchange of letters after the son's return from the war. After his discharge from the army, Charles used the experience he had gained in wool classification to acquire a post as a wool classer working for a firm called, coincidentally, F.W. Hughes. Like Bill he asked for his father's help in getting a job, help which was readily given. By 1924, he was working for Houghton and Company, a firm based in Auckland, New Zealand, and wrote to his father saying that the firm wished him to settle there, though he wanted to experience a winter in the country before deciding.

This he did, and kept his father informed of his progress and the vicissitudes of the wool trade as well as keeping him abreast of his love life and its occasional vicissitudes as well; he reported that he had fallen for a Miss Lamb but the similarity of their names had become the butt of too many jokes so he had fled the amatorial jousting ground. Hughes replied: 'I read the sad story of poor Miss Lamb. What is the world coming to when a poor girl's whole life can be spoiled because of her name. Ah well, watch out young feller my lad that some designing hussy doesn't gather you into her net and make you rue the day when you rejected Lamb with or without mint sauce.' Charles also sought his father's advice on business decisions, the state of the world and investments; in July 1925 he sent his father a cheque for £107.17.6 with a request for Hughes to invest it in war bonds for him. Hughes duly obliged and wrote congratulating his son on the way he was facing life, adding that to encourage him he would make up the sum to be invested to £200 out of his own pocket.

Shortly after the sad tale of Miss Lamb, Charles wrote to say that he was going to get married to a certain Margaret who was quite resigned to her impending fate, and that his golf had improved, though whether there was a relation between the two was left unsaid; he still agreed with the man who said that golf was not a game but a disease. The nuptials were delayed, however, when his sister Lily fell ill and he was obliged to assume part of the burden of payments for her medical treatment. He conveyed this state of affairs to his father, adding in his customary fashion brief bits of information — the wool trade was in a state of depression, his firm had hired a new assistant ('A typical young Englishman, rosy cheeks, a great opinion of himself, rather too verbose for my liking'). It was not until July 1928 that the marital knot was eventually spliced.

Lily had moved to New Zealand to be close to Charles, who continually demonstrated great affection, concern and responsibility in her regard. She was once written of in the Melbourne *Punch* as having passed the London College of Music piano examination, and a schoolbook of hers from 1900 shows beautiful handwriting, neat arithmetic sums, homework in transcription, science and analysis, and some banal poetry. She never married and depended entirely on the regular monies received from her father and Charles. She had always been a sickly child but became seriously ill in 1925, losing the use of her limbs from paralysis of the spine and requiring the constant attention of a nurse. Hughes had made regular payments to her over the years but now to meet the costs of her treatment a greater and more frequent outlay of money was required, with the likelihood that she would never recover fully. Charles contributed much himself and was insistent and persistent in squeezing additional support from his father, sometimes admonishing him for being tardy in responding, or pointing out: 'I know that you have a lot of expense with other members of the family but surely they can do with less than Lily can'.

Another daughter, Dolly, also depended on her father for regular disbursements: a typical letter came from 1 Eurona Flats, North Steyne Ocean Beach, Manly, though she lived most of her life in Melbourne: 'My Dear Dad, No doubt you have been so very busy you have forgotten to send my cheque. I know you must be frightfully rushed but as it is now the 7th I thought I'd give you a reminder as I have no money at all. Ethel told me about the trip to Java Dad and I can't realise it yet ... I have always longed to go to other countries and every time you went to England I hoped that you would take me just once. I wish you would come out and see us after the elections, it is not much use seeing you at your office for every time I go in they say you are very busy and make me feel that I am an interloper instead of your daughter.' These themes were to be repeated regularly in letters to her father. Another frequent reference was to her hopes that Hughes would come to see her pottery exhibition and wishes that he would accept one of her pieces made especially for him, on one occasion writing rather plaintively: 'it is more than a year since you said you would'. She kept him informed of her illnesses and the extent of her expenses for doctor's visits. Could she go on a holiday, she once pleaded, and elicited £20 from her 'Dada', thanking him for the 'lovely letter' which had accompanied the cheque.

Charles' pleas on behalf of Lily became sharper in the late twenties when Hughes was taken up with attacks on the Bruce Government and was, in Charles' eyes, excessively late in responding to his requests on Lily's behalf: 'still no word from you. I can't understand your attitude.' He spelled out Lily's situation: she had moved to Christchurch, which was less hilly and therefore easier for her to move around, she received £2 6d from her father but had expenses of £4 2d per week (Charles gave her £5 a month), and she was in debt for £20: 'She is helpless. Unlike other members of my family she has always been loyal to you. I'm not melodramatic but the situation is bad.' His next letter reported that he had heard from Lily, who had received the cheque Hughes had sent her for £25: 'As for Dorothy and Ethel I have not heard or seen either of them for at least two years and I know them both better than to think they would agree to do without anything.'

The gadfly

Amidst all this family turmoil, Hughes' day job was keeping him quite busy. His machinations against the Bruce-Page administration occasioned a degree of frostiness in his relations with Murdoch, who sent an admonishment to his staff: 'We should be careful of W.M. Hughes. His motives are ugly — vindictiveness, jealousy and self-interest. His dominant idea is not to help the country but to destroy Bruce.'[1] Bruce himself had written to Hughes in July 1925: 'Members of the party and many outside are greatly disturbed at the attitude you have taken up. They even go so far as to say that you are disgruntled and annoyed because you are not in my place.' This was no doubt the case, but threatening Hughes with loss of endorsement, which Hughes alleged Bruce was doing, would hardly have improved matters.

At the National Party Conference of 1928 Hughes threw a cat among the pigeons by expounding the view that the White Australia Policy should be extended to races other than from Eastern Asia, that is, applied to Southern Europeans as well: 'I believe there are too many Southern Europeans coming into this country. It is an alarming state of affairs. Let Italy have her place in the sun, but not here with our permission.' This provoked an attack on his position especially by Holman and Sir Neville Howse, the PM's spokesman; Hughes was out of the room during the onslaught but, returning, listened to others attack him, chewing gum incessantly and furiously scribbling notes. 'His eventual speech was a masterpiece', according to *The Sun*, which had reported him as having said: 'Good God Is there no end to this relationship? To whom does this country belong, to us or to Mussolini? Are we to be subservient to the Dago?' (Hughes denied using the term 'dago'.) This was in the context of a belief that the government had signed an immigration agreement with Italy allowing family members to join Italian relations already in Australia, a number estimated as being of the order of 300 per month: 'I do not assert our superiority but it is for us to develop our ideals along our own lines.' He also attacked negros in highly racist terms and expressed caustic views on America's contribution to the war effort; of an American war film he said, 'It was a beautiful war picture all about American aeroplanes and guns but it was as much like the facts as I am like Cleopatra. America did not have any guns and the planes could be packed under this platform.'

Almost as if to exemplify what a mixed bag of a man he was, after this episode redolent with racism he made one of his rare references to the traditional peoples of Australia, which suggested that he was ahead of his time in their regard. Exhibiting his persistent radicalism, which remained undimmed through the years, he wrote:

> It was never my good fortune to get into close touch with the rightful owners of this wonderful country but I like them and want to do all in my power to help them ... I often wish they had one or two representatives in the Federal Parliament. Given a fair show they would hold their own and ventilate their grievances, and perhaps even shame the community into extending the rights and privileges of citizenship, which we enjoy in such ample measure, to the descendants of the rightful owners of Australia.

The only other reference to indigenous Australians in his papers was his meeting with a 'black gin' during his early days tramping the byways of Queensland.

He was also much taken with constitutional issues and the changes needed to bolster the strength of the Federation. He anticipated current debate in Australia and elsewhere regarding the right balance between central and devolved authority, and looked at the dilution of state powers and even the possible abolition of state parliaments, state politicians and state governors. He regarded the Australian currency of his day antiquated and in need of radical change, and thought the continued use of Imperial weights and measures as equally antiquated. He believed too that the government of the day was bent on jettisoning all that had been painfully won over to federal control and returning powers to the states — an almost eerie antecedent of newspaper coverage of such issues in 2005.

For Hughes, nationalism had 'become the servile tool of great vested interests. Bruce cannot carry on ... His finance is rotten, he has no policy, at best he just drifts. Every day he is in strengthens labour, and as long as labour is honeycombed by the Reds, a Labour Government is not to be desired'.[2] Barely a month later Hughes did bring about the fall of Bruce by moving an amendment to the Maritime Industries Bill which was won by one vote. The government resigned, and no doubt for Hughes there was in it an element of sweet revenge. The issue for the government's defeat was reform of the Arbitration Court, which Bruce wanted to scrap. However Hughes' antipathy to the Bruce government was of longer standing and not merely a matter of sour grapes for having been removed from office; in 1927 the government had announced its intention to sell the Commonwealth Shipping Line. For Hughes, who had created the Shipping Line, this smacked of fundamental betrayal and, although it was eventually sold, his attack in Parliament rattled the government and led to the final showdown over the Arbitration Court.

In defence of his action Hughes argued: 'I was elected to support certain principles ... [the] impartial administration of justice, and compulsory arbitration. Both are planks of the Nationalist Party Platform and have been there since I founded it. Which am I to follow — the leader who turns his back on our platform or the principles to which I subscribed before the people?' The director general of the Nationalist campaign entered the fray to argue that Hughes was not the founder of the party, that it was Holman and Wade. This claim was subsequently shown to be erroneous when a letter from Hughes was produced and quoted showing that he indeed was the founder, having sent the letter inviting various personages to a meeting in the Melbourne Town Hall on Tuesday 9 January 1917 which resulted in the Nationalist Federation being established.

One result of the government's fall and Hughes' part in bringing it down was that the Killara Golf Club 'sent him to Coventry' to show their disapproval, with only one member, a retired hardware merchant, prepared to play with him. Faces at the club were somewhat reddened in September 1932 when Hughes was made an honorary member of the St Andrews Golf Club in Scotland — a rare honour.

The domestic scene, again

A glimpse of domestic life at Elderslie in these years was given by a journalist from *The Age* who had been sent to the house to collect a copy of a speech Hughes was to deliver in Chatworth on 2 December 1929: 'When I arrived, the door of the drawing room was open and he [Hughes] had his back to it seated at a little table playing solo or bridge. Mrs Hughes came to the door with a yelping poodle and told me to go to another front door — and she then went around and opened it and ushered me into a cosy sitting room.' Joe Gullett, Hughes' friend and a relation of Mary, said that Hughes would frequently sit on the veranda only in his underpants.

A greater degree of domesticity developed in his relations with his eldest son Bill and family, whom he saw regularly during parliamentary sessions now that they were held in Canberra. According to a granddaughter, Bill sought to become a Parliamentary Hansard note-taker at one point but decided that his shorthand was not good enough, though he could take dictation using Pitman shorthand at 150 words per minute. Eventually with his father's help he joined the Department of Government looking after Canberra's parks and gardens. Every week Hughes senior would come to Bill's house for a meal with the family and on leaving would always slip a few coins into the children's pockets. On one occasion the younger son, who had been asleep, woke when Hughes was about to leave and stuck his hand out: 'Nothing for you my lad', said Grandpa, 'only for those who stay awake'. Bill's children would on occasion visit their grandfather in his grand house in Lindfield. If Dame Mary were there she would not allow them in by the front door but escort them round to the back to the tradesmen's entrance.

Familial concerns

Diana Williams, Hughes' great-granddaughter, recalled that Bill enjoyed good relations with his father, although a hiatus of some two years occurred over a political disagreement when Bill became involved in local politics in Canberra and was secretary of the Labor Party for some years. The temporary rupture in relations may have been due to Bill taking a leading role in Canberra on behalf of the local party against the government's Unlawful Assemblies Ordinance. Though never rich, Bill lived a long and reasonably comfortable life in Kingston, where he died at the age of 89.

The fortunes of Hughes' children over the Tasman were little changed, Charles writing regularly with views on both the state of the wool trade and the world, and occasional news of other members of the first family. There would seem to have been a close bond between the children and there is testimony that they corresponded at irregular intervals, Charles on one occasion complaining to his father that he had not heard from Bill for nearly two years: 'he and I as you know have always been bosom companions'. Increasingly too his letters focused on the plight of Lily: could his father please give her some more support 'to help her along life's roadway'. It was more than likely that brother and sister combined in putting pressure on Hughes, for often Lily's letters echoed her brother's even to the extent of using the same words and phrases. A letter from her in January 1929 followed almost an identical one from Charles asking her father to please send her a cheque: the state of her spine was such that she could not lift anything, she was not extravagant, she had not bought any clothes all year except for a woolly costume against the cold. At the end of the month her father sent an instruction to his bank to forward £25 to her. Lily responded with many thanks. She believed she was improving: she could now get about but only on the flat and could walk for 20 minutes. She said that Charlie was to be a father in August. His new wife, Margaret wrote thanking Hughes for 'his beautiful gift'.

A year later a letter arrived from solicitors in Christchurch noting that Lily received £10 per month, which with other remittances brought what she received in total to £4 per week. Could this be assured? In succeeding months plaintive pleas come from Lily: 'I can't live on what you send me ... from your afflicted daughter ... Chuck [Charles] sends me help. You used to love me Dad and although you won't believe me I would love to love you and have you for a real father — one who really cares, I mean. Please send cheque by cable — I just can't live on 2 pound 6 shillings a week'. Charles wrote to make the same point, then at the end of May another plea comes from Lily: 'I am an invalid. Please understand. Will you provide for my future. I am afraid. To be stuck in an institution, how dreadful that would be, your sick daughter.' This was typical of Hughes — keeping those who depended on his largesse at the end of a tight string, doling out his offerings piecemeal.

Chapter 12

Back to the fray

James Scullin won the 1929 election for Labor following the fall of the Bruce Government and served as Prime Minister until 1931. This period saw almost as great a divide in the party as encountered by Hughes over conscription, due to a combination of economic recession and internal party disputes. Hughes wrote: 'Mr Scullin failed because he had no power and because he had no courage to reach out for the power.'

Twiddling his thumbs

During his wilderness years from office Hughes was once described by R.J. Bernays, an English journalist visiting Parliament at the time, as the 'loneliest figure in Australian public life, without power and party'. 'Solitary' would have been a more accurate description, for throughout these times there were always those ready either to engage him in debate, seek his advice or listen to his stories. He remained ever his own man: 'he did not pose, he did not truckle to the mob nor did he bend the knee to great interests'. To an extent he was cocooned by his deafness and protected from the temptations of too close conviviality by the rigours of his largely solitary upbringing — his mother dying when he was six years old, being farmed out to relatives for seven years, entering lodgings at the age of 12, emigrating to the other end of the world at 22, tramping the empty Queensland bush alone, taking on the toughest working men of the Sydney dockyards, and knuckling his way into the hurly burly of political life.

Billy Hughes

He had begun to champ at the bit, believing that further greatness on the grand political stage was still his for the taking. His initial foray back into the fray, however, had been short-lived: he became very involved in the creation of a new party, the Australia Party, which held its first convention on 19 April 1930 and agreed a constitution as well as a policy platform. The convention also agreed to support the Scullin Government as long as it acted wisely. But Hughes' heart was not entirely in it and in 1932 he joined the United Australia Party — the renascent Nationalist Party of Prime Minister Joseph Lyons, which had come to power the previous December.

In the 1932 election campaign, Hughes was attacked in highly derogatory terms by his opponents. Standing against him was a Dr Noh, who received a letter of support from a firm of stockbrokers enclosing a cheque 'to help you exterminate Australia's worst political rat' (i.e. Hughes). Noh's electoral propaganda included a message from an old digger: 'ever since the war [Hughes] has worked the returned soldier and "little digger" stunt, until it has become nauseating'. This was an oft-repeated jibe by his enemies, of standing in the reflected glory of the Australian soldier. The attacks had little electoral effect, for Hughes was returned with a majority of 12 969 votes.

He left Melbourne on 31 May 1932 with Mary and Helen aboard the *Oronsay* for a holiday in England. In one speech there Hughes recounted the time when he had been given the freedom of the City of London and had asked the then Lord Mayor what privileges the 'freedom' accorded him. The Lord Mayor, somewhat nonplussed, sent one of his officials to seek an answer and on returning informed Hughes a trifle red-faced that he had the right to graze one cow on the public common. Hughes also paid what was to be his last visit to Llandudno, playing two games of golf — one at the Great Orme and the other at Maesdu.

He delivered various other speeches, including one on Empire trade in Edinburgh, but his sojourn in Britain was truncated when a cable came from Lyons asking him to act as the second member of the Australian delegation to the League of Nations Assembly to be held in

Geneva — Bruce to be the leader. Press comment wondered how the two men could work together, though one report had Hughes exhibiting his chameleon capacity acting with 'sweetness of manner in recent months'. His comments on some of those attending the conference were not so jocund: 'In time of depression, economists multiply like fleas on a dunghill'. One participant — the Irish representative Mr De Valera — found Hughes sensible, and much admired his opening speech. In September, Bruce wrote to him apologising he had been delayed, leaving him in the lurch. In fact, Hughes led the delegation for the whole of the conference except for two days. The family returned on the *Oronsay* on 12 November and Hughes unveiled the war memorial for the fallen Australian and New Zealand servicemen in Port Said on the 23rd of the month. He received a warm letter of salutation from King Faisal, whom he had met at the Peace Conference when Lawrence of Arabia had acted as interpreter — an unnecessary service since the King spoke good English.

Hughes admitted on one occasion that by and large he chose his secretaries for their looks not their brains, but on return to Australia he acquired a new secretary who was well endowed with both attributes and was to prove more remarkable and durable than most. Dorothy Beryl Mahomed was the daughter of Shah Mahomed of Lahore and an English mother, Jane Davies, and stayed with Hughes for over seven years. She was recorded as living on the corner of Durville Crescent and Stokes Street in Griffith, Canberra, in 1940 when Malcolm Booker was the head of Hughes' private office. She subsequently, in 1941, went to work for Robert Menzies, a move regarded by Hughes as treachery (though, years later, she was espied entering the visitors section of Parliament by Hughes while in the middle of a speech; the old man interrupted his flow, walked over to where she sat, gave her a warm embrace, and returned to continue his oration).

She recounted to her daughter Patricia how working for Hughes, though turbulent at times, was infinitely more rewarding compared to her stint with Menzies, adversely comparing Menzies' 'pomposity' with Hughes' 'lightness of being'. They obviously worked well together, with Hughes baptising her with a pet name, Saruya. On one occasion when Mary came to her husband's room she found him changing his clothes for the formal dinner they were about to attend: 'I've promised Miss Mahomed that I would always turn my back when she has to change and she agreed to do to the same for me'. Dorothy Mahomed was an accomplished musician and a gifted amateur actress, gifts that found a sympathetic resonance with Hughes. When they were travelling by car, a tartan rug over their knees, they would punctuate the journey with quotes from Shakespeare and songs from London musicals. Along with frequent renderings of 'Alas poor Yorick, I knew him', Hughes would sing 'Saruya was handsome. Saruya was fair. She lived down the lane near Bloomsbury Square.' She played tennis frequently at The Lodge, the Prime Minister's residence, and was well regarded by the Lyons family. She would tell her daughter of the various incidents in the office, how Hughes would always have numerous scraps of paper with him on which he would scribble memos and ideas as they came to him, and then leave them in a pile for his secretary to make sense of. On the election of an opponent he once remarked to her: 'He's got a secret weapon — a young and beautiful wife, and I've only got bloody Mary'. Saruya would get very upset at how he treated his wife, but came to realise that it was more bark than bite.

Up front again

By May 1933, Murdoch's relations with his erstwhile friend had improved, with Murdoch writing 'My dear Wm' and sending his warm regards. In November of the next year Murdoch sent a telegram strongly urging him to re-enter the political firmament and take a position in the Lyons Government, which Hughes did, becoming Minister of State for Health and Repatriation after 12 years on the backbenches. Francis Forde, then the Deputy Leader of the ALP, wrote to congratulate him on his appointment and received a not untypical reply from Hughes enjoining him to 'take good and evil with unruffled front … take all in your stride', a sentiment which one suspects was certainly one of the engines which propelled himself through both the years of great success and the fallow years from his unseating as Prime Minister to his return to the front bench. Forde returned the compliment, writing that although they were on different sides of politics Hughes was to be congratulated for doing what neither Clemenceau nor Lloyd George had achieved — succeeding in making a political comeback.

Despite an operation to have his appendix out, followed by pneumonia late in 1934, Hughes' energy remained undiminished. Though also being very busy as Minister for Health (this was when he had three secretaries as a result of the new pension legislation), his years in the Lyons administration seem to have been particularly happy ones as far as he was concerned. Others thought that he was a constant nuisance in cabinet but Lyons liked him and defended giving him a portfolio on the basis that it was preferable putting up with him close at hand rather than have him making mischief on the backbenches. Hughes, however, could still come up with the telling put-down or caustic phrase, such as his comment on possible public reaction to the 1934 budget surplus: 'people don't care a tinker's damn about any surplus save their own. What shall it profit a man if the Treasury burst with gold if we are on the dole.'

For Menzies, Hughes had become 'primarily reminiscent' by the end of 1934, as he wrote in his *Afternoon Light*, but on another occasion commented, 'unpredictable he could be but dull he couldn't be if he tried'. Hughes continued to spell sudden death to all pomposity and humbug. He was proud of the Lyons Government's achievements and recorded what he regarded as the most important: reduced taxation, reduced income tax, the abolition of the entertainment tax, reduced average interest charges per annum, reduced unemployment.

The Hughes and Lyons families got on well together and saw each other often, especially during parliamentary sessions in Canberra. Hughes, however, remained ever the radical and there was a brief parting of the ways over Hughes' views published in a small volume entitled 'Australia and War Today', calling for Australia to rearm. He argued that the rule of law depended on force and the League of Nations had none and could in no way defend Australia if she was attacked: 'The League is powerless. It talks, it appeals, it supplicates, it negotiates, it cannot act.' For Hughes, therefore, the League had been a failure, the United Kingdom was not strong and only France and Russia would be on its side in the event of war; German rearmament was a greater menace to world peace than Italy's invasion of Abyssinia.

War, in Hughes' mind, was a recurring phenomenon, and war and peace were but phases in an eternal struggle for existence, trade and territory. The weak were always in the wrong and only the weak had no enemies; sanctions could only be effective if backed by armed force. Later he was to write, 'There is peace only by the grace of God and the fact that the United States has the Atomic Bomb'. An article in the *Herald* in December 1933 by Sir Thomas Henley attacked Hughes for his 'war-mongering ... I am more than willing to make generous allowance for the strange combustible mixture that generates the power so evident in your erratic political movements, and for your capricious oscillations in response to every quake in the political world.'

One result of the publication of 'Australia and War Today' was that Lyons felt obliged to demand Hughes' resignation, since the cabinet was in favour of sanctions against Italy whereas his book stated that such moves were irrelevant: 'either an empty gesture or war'. In his reply to Lyons, Hughes wrote that the request to resign was a surprise and a shock, and the reference to sanctions was but a couple of sentences: 'I do not and can not feel enthusiasm about the efficiency of economic sanctions but I agree that their imposition now constitutes the only practical contribution that Great Britain the Dominions and the League of Nations can agree upon.' Of the League he said: 'I welcome the League of Nations but does anyone think the League will bottle up human nature?' He once characterised moral force as 'trying to prevent a hungry tiger springing on its prey by offering him a tract on vegetarianism'. Hughes' subsequent resignation was short-lived, though he replied to one correspondent that, like Brer Rabbit, he was 'laying low'. He returned to the cabinet some months later, having received support for his reappointment from Murdoch, Amery, old diggers and assorted voices. Hughes then passed what he described as a Dickens Christmas — 'white wet and wonderful' — including a trip to Sassafras and a splendid time with the Murdochs at Cruden Farm in Frankston where Lady Elizabeth, Murdoch's wife, had recently been delivered of a 'lovely new baby'.

In 1934, he was almost alone in arguing that the perceived threat from Japan was infinitely more menacing for Australia, and fought a solitary fight to increase air protection against what he believed to be an imminent attack by this country. He and Lyons also had differing views on the Dominion Office in London, which Hughes felt was quite useless: 'as out of date as the hansom cab'. What he wanted was direct access by Australia to the Foreign Office, a position strongly supported by the ALP, which welcomed his advocacy in this regard, one comment being: 'Hughes is a political catalyst'. A year later saw a renewed Department of External Affairs in Canberra, though the opening of Australian diplomatic posts in North America and Asia had to wait for a further five years. He also protested vigorously when Lyons sent an official telegram of support to Chamberlain, which Hughes felt could be seen as condoning Hitler's actions, and never missed an opportunity to ridicule Chamberlain's appeasement policy.

In the midst of all, Hughes kept up with his connections in Britain. The Welsh philanthropist Lord Davies of Llandinam, who had read 'Australia and War Today', sent him some of his own views and wondered whether Hughes would become vice-president of a group aiming to set up an international system for dispute settlement and an organised system of sanctions. He also pointed out that Llandinam was only some 30 miles away from Llansantffraid in Montgomeryshire and forwarded to Hughes a copy of a book entitled *Montgomeryshire Worthies*. Davies had inherited considerable wealth from his grandfather, who had made his money from coalmines, especially in the Rhondda, had built Barry Docks in South Wales, and was one of the foremost movers in establishing the University College of Wales in Aberystwyth. The grandson had been a strong supporter of the League of Nations and had fought in the trenches in World War I.

There was irregular correspondence between Hughes and Davies over the years, including a beautiful document produced for the opening of the Welsh Temple of Peace and Health on 23 November 1938 as a memorial to those of all nations who had lost their lives fighting for their country. Lord Davies wrote asking Hughes along with other prominent Welshmen for donations towards the Shrine: was it possible to receive two exhibition cases, two tables and chairs of Australian walnut for a total cost of £113 pounds three shillings and sixpence? At the official opening of the Temple of Peace a message was read from Hughes and from Charles Evans Hughes, the Chief Justice of the Supreme Court of the USA. It was also Lord Davies who provided the money for the establishment of the first ever chair of International Politics at the University College of Wales Aberystwyth. The Chair is named the Wilson Chair after the US President and the person who persuaded Lord Davies to choose Aberystwyth rather than Oxford for the endowment was another Welshman, Thomas Jones appointed by Lloyd George as Deputy Secretary of his Cabinet on becoming Prime Minister in 1916.

Mixed blessings

On the family front, Arthur, who saw his stepfather from time to time, prior to meeting Hughes in November 1934 wrote: 'many, many thanks for all your kindnesses'. He had applied for a job and enclosed a copy of his application showing that he was 47 years old, a public accountant and secretary, graduate of Stotts Business College, honorary secretary of the United Charities Fund, and a member of the firm of Hughes and Ball. Among his referees was a J.W. Packer. He informed his stepfather that the family had moved to 2 Canberra Court, Glenayr Avenue, Seven Ways, Bondi. Later his wife Mabel wrote to Hughes that her daughter Gwen was still very ill in Delaware Hospital and thanked him for helping Arthur get a job: 'I hope you will not mind us saying Gwen was your grand daughter, we do not trade on this as a rule, as you mainly saved her life if she recovers.' Gifts from Hughes came regularly at Christmas and birthdays: on one occasion, silk stockings for the two girls, slippers for Mabel.

Sometime in 1934 Charles wrote with alarming news that Lily had suffered a breakdown and had been taken to a mental home in Auckland, and that she had threatened to commit suicide and to make some public disclosures (unspecified). No doubt this referred to the same grievances and threats Ethel had made some ten years earlier. Hughes replied by cable and forwarded money to help. By January 1935, Lily had improved and Charles wrote that he had taken her to his home in Wellington. Hughes again forwarded £25 to help with the medical bills. In October, Charles wrote that he did not think he would get advancement in the wool business and that he should perhaps be going into business for himself. In April 1936 he was still in the wool trade and it was picking up.

Hughes kept copies of masses of letters received and sent during this period asking for his intervention in a variety of matters: help for disabled gassed veterans, selling a house for an old digger, pension settlements, appointments, honours. He helped the widow of a deceased explorer, dealt with dismissals from the public service, was asked to support a way to destroy Australia's curse (the prickly pear), handled questions regarding tariffs on gold leaf, found jobs for people on the coastal steamers and was deluged with a plethora of demands for his intervention to prevent Canberra from acquiring a liquor licence! One of the few personal diaries with much of interest is that of 1935: much travelling, Cabinet sessions, race meetings, conferences (on such matters as 'The Need for a Health Certificate before Marriage'), garden parties, United Australia Party meetings, and speeches. One letter came from his old friend Ben Tillett from Transport House in London, who asked whether Australians were becoming more 'Yankee' than ever. If so it was a menace to civilisation in general and to Australia in particular. Hughes replied that he did not think so, although they were more Australianised than they had been.

In the same year Sir Norman Cowper, who had stood against Hughes in the North Sydney constituency in the 1931 election, paid him a visit in Lindfield and wrote of a small incident when Hughes, going into his study to look for some papers, shouted 'Mary, Mary'; a small reply came from the kitchen, 'Yes William?' 'Did you see the manuscript I was working on?' 'No William. I tidied that room this morning and may have moved it.' Turning to Cowper, Hughes expostulated: 'Goddam it Cowper. If that woman ever goes to heaven there will be no resurrection. Oh no. She'll tidy the place up and the Angel Gabriel will lose his trumpet.'

The year 1936 was one of dramatic incident: in February Hughes was admitted to the Jenner Hospital at Potts Point for an operation for appendicitis. On the 14th of the month the *Herald* carried a headline: 'Mr Hughes keeps a secretary for more than nine months' (a Mr Connell). A week later he and two friends were involved in yet another motor accident, this time in Albury skidding on loose gravel. He spoke to the Melbourne Savage Club in May 1936, though due to a colossal printing error the poster advertising the talk bore not his picture but that of some nurses with babies! When he was to be present at any such social event with his wife he wrote 'Dame Mary' invariably, never just 'Mary'. In June, Mary wrote to her friend Hilda Abbott: 'he certainly had a very narrow escape and I am thankful things were not as bad as they might have been.' This was apropos a plane crash, with Hughes again suffering a broken collarbone (not, in this rare case, due to him being at the wheel).

Back in the saddle

Elections were held in October 1936 and Hughes was appointed Minister for Territories in the new government. He immediately involved himself in the vexed question of whether Rabaul should remain the capital of New Guinea or a new site be chosen. He visited Papua New Guinea and wrote a very readable, if colonialist, account of the trip: 'I like these people, they are friendly cheerful souls who respond to decent treatment.' He never wavered from the view he had enunciated at the Paris Peace Conference that control of New Guinea was essential to the freedom and indeed to the very existence of Australia. However, as far as immigration was concerned, he remained a dyed-in-the-wool believer in keeping Australia white, and this to him basically meant the

English-speaking peoples. Prior to his outburst against further Italian immigrants, while Prime Minister, he had tried to keep a boatload of Maltese from landing in Australia but had to yield to public opinion, which was greatly sympathetic to Malta as a result of the staunch support and aid given to Anzacs by the Maltese during the war.

At the same time he was conscious that the population of Australia had to increase, as evinced in his 'populate or perish' campaigning. Hughes was keen to take a well-informed view in the debate and requested a report in this regard from Chas. H. Wicken, the Commonwealth statistician. The report outlined the growth of the population since colonisation, from '0' in 1788 (obviously disregarding the original inhabitants), through the gold rush boom and the great increases between 1911 and 1920. The report also examined the density of population in 1939 compared to that of more populous countries of the world — with Australia on 2.5 persons per square mile, the UK on 508 and Holland up to 679.5.

In December of the same year, Hughes received many letters praising an article in the *Sydney Morning Herald* and speeches regarding the possible abdication of Edward VIII. The *Canberra Times* reported on: 'the signal honour given him' in being invited to King Edward's coronation. Edward, as Prince of Wales, had visited Australia in May 1920 and was not greeted with universal acclaim; Hughes was to write of his 'horror and indignation at the cowardly and dastardly treatment by the crowd gathered to greet the Prince'. For Hughes the Royal Family was the lynchpin of the Empire, though there is little evidence in his conduct or writings of the gushing forelocking later exhibited by Menzies.

Various contemporaries mentioned the Hughes' sojourns at the hotel Canberra for Parliamentary sessions, especially Fadden and Dame Enid Lyons, the latter often sharing a table with them for dinner. According to her, Hughes, at this stage, was a man of determined habits, always having breakfast in his room and invariably rising from the dining room at 8 pm to go to the billiard table: 'where his skill, not great, outshone his sportsmanship, the purpose of the game was to win.' She also noted that he clung to the old mode of address — 'Mr, Mrs, Sir, Lady' — and usually prefaced every remark with 'Ah' (similarly, one of his favourite introductory phrases was 'The position as I see it is ...'). Even at 80 years of age, she later observed, 'he walked with a springy step, talked with zest and an ever ready wit ... His dress was always immaculate.' It was Dame Enid who on 9 May 1964 did the honours and unveiled the memorial plaque to Hughes in the Canberra suburb named after him.

While in Canberra Hughes was a frequent purchaser of goods from a Welsh chemist in Kingston named John L. Davies. An example of typical purchases over a two-week period included: Enos fruit salts, methylated spirits, paraffin oil, soap, mixture, Napro, Aspro. He also made frequent purchases of barley sugar, of which he was inordinately fond, used an inhaler and was an avid reader of the *Listener*.

Chapter 13

Helen — a shadow fell

If 1916 had been Hughes' annus mirabilis, 1937 was his annus horribilis. A child of Hughes' comparative old age — he was 53 when she was born — his daughter Helen Beatrice Myfanwy became his darling bud of May and his 'gleam of eternal sunshine'. In all his vast accumulation of papers almost the only examples of Hughes expressing deep emotion in respect of any individual come in references to his daughter Helen, born in 1916 and baptised in Ashford Kent by one Frank Edinger. The papers include bundles of notes and letters from Helen to her father and a few from him to her, often undated, which show that the relationship was equally warm in her regard for him. An interesting view of her father came in an article she wrote entitled 'What I Think of My Father', in which she said that he combined the sublime and the ridiculous, that he didn't mind the frequent cartoons featuring him, and that 'if he gets cross with me I just lift him up: he is very little'.[1]

Some letters were written when she was very young, the earliest coming from Hampstead to Hughes at the Paris Peace Conference when she was barely five years of age. As the years passed by her letters reflected the excitement of growing up, early enthusiasms, childish pride ('Don't I write beautifully Pappa'). Several letters are written in excellent French, a language facility her father never failed to encourage; however, a school report from Marshall Mount School said that, while her oral and spoken French was good, her written French left something to be desired. Other school reports from her time at Marshall Mount and Abbotsleigh schools sometimes note that she was adjusting well and they look forward to her continuing to make good progress; still others suggest that she was too talkative and should apply herself more diligently. She regaled her father with news of the people she met and the visits she made, to the theatre to see a play she called 'the Twelfth Night', to a cocktail party at the Drake-Brockmans, to Sassafras, which she loved. The tone of the letters is always bright and cheerful; she was, at eleven, writing a play entitled 'Where Cupid's Arrow Goes', she enthused about new experiences, and her world seemed full of wonder. However, like her mother Mary and Hughes' other children, Helen, for all that she was the apple of her father's eye, still had to remind him at regular intervals that he had been negligent or tardy in forwarding her allowance. She also upbraided him when he had not written for some time.

In one of the few letters on record from Hughes to Helen he began in French: 'Ma petite Mignonne' ('My little Darling') and employed a style and language befitting the age of his daughter, quite different from the often stilted prose he used in correspondence with adults. The language is simple and direct, light and airy: one letter begins with 'I play golf every day' then goes on to recount how he also played at foxes and badgers and rabbits with the Deanes' daughter. He enjoyed being in the presence of children; the photographs at the National Library of Australia include a number with him more relaxed and smiling in their presence than in most other circumstance, and the attraction would seem to have been mutual. Small children seemed to find in this frail and ugly man a directness and warmth, unfeigned and unstilted, sensing one who without pretence or condescension enjoyed their company.

Whenever possible Hughes would ensure that Helen accompanied him and Dame Mary on their travels: to Britain as a babe in arms in 1916 and again as a child four years later; to the US in 1924 when she was looked after by a governess at the Hotel Alta Mira in Sausalito, California, while her father went on a speaking tour. When the Federal Parliament moved from Melbourne to Canberra in 1927, Helen often came with her parents for the duration of the parliamentary sessions. In the early days there was no suitable school for her to attend and again a governess was provided for her, as well as for a Canberra friend, Del Calthorpe, who lived in number

24 Mugga Way just a few yards away from the plot of land which Hughes had purchased but never developed. In 1932, she returned once more to Europe with her parents; a photograph taken of the family aboard the *Aronsay* when docked in Colombo shows a teenager of surpassing beauty. The *Canberra Times* later carried a photograph showing her in more formal attire but equally attractive when she attended a grand ball at Parliament House given in honour of the Duke of Gloucester and had the honour of being the Duke's first partner: 'she wore a gown of hydrangea blue satin with a little military cape of the same material falling from the shoulders'.

She seemed to enjoy good health and there are no references to her being in any way a sickly child, though on a few occasions there are indications that she might have been a trifle highly strung: one doctor's report described her as being run-down and nervy but that her parents were not to worry — what she needed was plenty of fresh air. Her mother did also on one occasion write to Hughes indicating concern with Helen's health, reporting that she had been in pain in the appendix region and that she had been advised to have an x-ray. Helen acknowledged a concern herself, writing to her father immediately prior to flying to Brisbane to take part in a mannequin parade for which she would receive 15 guineas plus expenses: 'My chief problem is nervousness ... not brought on by lack of attention from the opposite sex ...' There are no indications of Helen's boyfriends in Hughes' papers, though one as attractive as she would no doubt have had many admirers: a number of possible beaux would have been in attendance at a dance her parents gave for her 20th birthday at the Sydney Royal Yacht Squadron.

Shortly after her trip to Brisbane Helen set off once more for Britain, this time travelling alone on the Orient Company's ship, the *Oxford*, to arrive in Britain on 11 February 1937. Apropos the impending visit of his daughter, Hughes wrote to Lord Wakefield in England, a letter that in the light of later events can be regarded as extremely prescient or merely the normal effusion of a doting father concerned at his offspring's first trip alone over the oceans. Hughes informed Wakefield that Helen, now 21, would be attending the Coronation ceremonies later in the year: 'She is filled with gorgeous confidence', and then a jarring note: 'I am consumed with doubts and fears', with no further elucidation of what those doubts and fears might have been. He added that he would be grateful for anything Wakefield could do to help with her stay.

Helen wrote home regularly after her arrival in England from a house at Campden Hill, where she stayed for some time. Her letters, as usual, were chatty, recounting her experiences both mundane and interesting — on the one hand having two wisdom teeth extracted and on the other hand having tea with Mrs Neville Chamberlain. She had suffered painful stomach problems over the year and had been to see a specialist, a Dr Hurst, who had recommended she go on a diet as well as entering his clinic for three weeks for treatment. Her next letter came from New Lodge Clinic, Windsor Forest, Berkshire, suggesting she had taken the doctor's advice. In April she wrote from Freiburg in Germany before proceeding to Basel, Baden Baden ('a kind of German Monte Carlo') and Zurich, writing that she would be presented at court on 6 May. Her last dated letter to her father was sent from the Curzon House Club in Mayfair, in which she reported that after being presented at court she had gone to The Savoy for dinner with 'John'. Other undated letters from Helen to her 'Daddy' and to others during her stay in London include one to a Mrs Hordern saying she had to see her as soon as possible to discuss something very important. In late July she spoke to her mother by wireless telephone.

On 9 August 1937, Hughes had just arrived in Mildura, where he was to attend the city's jubilee celebrations, when his world collapsed with the devastating news that his beloved daughter had died at Beversbrook Nursing Home in Brondesbury, London. She had just turned 22 years of age. According to the *Melbourne Herald*, death had occurred during an acute abdominal operation, whereas the *Sydney Morning Herald* reported that it had followed an operation for a perforated duodenal ulcer. Some descendants of Hughes believed the cause of death was a botched abortion, though close friends of Dame Mary knew the truth: Helen had indeed become pregnant, with conception having occurred in Australia. Aware of her condition and to avoid a likely scandal if the news had emerged, her parents had sent her to England to have the baby delivered. This may have been what Hughes had in mind in his somewhat gnomic letter to Lord Wakefield. They also knew that a baby boy was born and that Helen died giving birth, not from an abortion, and that Hughes left £5000 in his will for the child's upbringing. Diane Langmore wrote that Helen 'died in childbirth after a caesarian section in a London nursing home'[2] but believed the parents were not aware of her pregnancy. The actual death certificate gives the cause of death as 'toxaemia from pelvic abscess following caesarian section for contraction pain after twenty four hours of labour'. The surgeon was one A.C. Palmer and the informant of the death was named as a certain Mr Hillon of Kilburn. Helen's address was given as the Curzon House Club, Curzon Street.

Helen's death was shocking to all who had known her but was a subject of intense sensitivity to her step-uncle Bill, who was inordinately fond of her and very deeply upset at her untimely passing. Helen had been a truly beautiful child and had grown into a personable young woman much admired and liked by all who knew her, including Pat Levy, a prominent Sydney lawyer, Keith Murdoch and numerous would-be swains. The unanswered question for the family then and the descendants today is the identity of the father of her child. Murdoch sent a warm letter of condolence to Hughes: 'I hope to see you soon. I am told that you think I neglect you. My dear friend I am a bad correspondent but a loyal and affectionate friend.' Sir Keith outlived Hughes by a matter of weeks only, dying in October 1952. He too had named one of his daughters Helen, who died in 1959.

There were numerous letters of condolence. A letter from Australia House included the sentence '... the medical officer in attendance has written you complete particulars and I have been advised that your wishes have had attention'. The writer was the deputy secretary, named Duffy. Bill wrote to his father, as did Dolly and Lily. Telegrams flooded in from Menzies (then Attorney General), Lyons the Prime Minister, Malcolm Macdonald, Harold Holt, Lloyd George, Earle Page and many others. One who also wrote was Archbishop Mannix, who sealed reconciliation with Hughes in a warm embrace when they next met. Obituaries remarked on her beauty, her fair hair, her popularity; how she would, whenever possible, go and listen to her father speaking, seeking an unobtrusive vantage point; how she enjoyed skiing; how the Duke of Gloucester had spent more time on the dance floor with her than with any other. The funeral saw a gathering of the political establishment of the country, including the Prime Minister and his wife. The body had been embalmed, placed in a hermetically sealed leaden shell with face glass, enclosed in an outer oaken casket, transferred to Tilbury Docks and loaded on to the steamship *Ormonde* for shipment to Sydney. She was buried in the Northern Suburbs Cemetery with the gravestone inscribed 'In loving memory of our darling daughter Helen Beatrice Myfanwy Hughes' and including her father's final salutation:

> Sleep on my love in thy cold bed
> Never to be disquieted
> Thou wilt not wake till I thy fate shall overtake
> Till age or grief or sickness must
> Marry my body to that dust
> It so much loves
> And show how'eer my marches be
> I shall at last sit down by thee.

Hughes' old friend and great admirer, Mary Gilmore, also wrote a poem in her honour:

> *In Memoriam*
> Here once she came in beauty like a flower
> The very winds her curtains were falling
> Like silver shifts about her feet when from
> His height the Austral sun looked down
> To mark which way her young glad feet had gone
> Lest as she went, too soon a shadow fell
> Upon the happy hours that were her lot
> Who here once came in beauty like a flower

In November of 1937 Hughes received a letter sent to Helen from solicitors in London asking for payment of £9 9s for a black evening dress supplied in May. There are no words of Hughes' to record his grief at what was the greatest tragedy of his life. One account had him locking himself in his room for four days then going back to his office exhibiting no outward change.[3] He also took long, secret drives in the car, including a drive with Dorothy Mahomed to see Mannix at his residence, Raheen, in Melbourne. Some years later in a letter of condolence to a Mr Carruthers on the loss of his child, Hughes wrote with the ring of truth: 'I too have known what it is to lose a child. I know therefore how idle is the well-intentioned consolation of friends. Time alone is the great consoler. Even he heals imperfectly. All else is mockery.'

More family trauma

The year 1937 also saw Lily confined to a convalescent home for more than a year before Charles wrote that she had improved sufficiently to leave the home but would never be able to earn a living. He suggested to Hughes that they consider buying a small house for her and perhaps rent out a spare room to another lady. Another forlorn missive came from Lily herself: 'Won't you help me get a holiday. I really am very depressed. I need a change. Life seems to be a very hard thing; if you don't help me a bit I don't think I'll bother much more. I'm all in. I really thought you meant to keep your word this time. I can't work very hard ever and now I feel that I'm at the end of my tether. Everything is so dear now, a day's rent alone takes more than you give me.' By December 1938 Hughes had put down a deposit of £120 pounds on a cottage for her. Lily was clearly joyful, with abundant thanks to her dear 'Dada' for her new home at 41 Peverel St, Riccarton. It had a 'wee' garden back and front, four rooms, pantry, bathroom, kitchen, wash house and spare room. There were two fireplaces and a gas stove. She had also acquired a 'wee dog'. Lily wrote again to say how happy she was in her own house, adding: 'life is very peculiar in New Zealand. Everyone gets high wages and old people big pensions yet everyone seems stony broke.'

Dolly wrote from St Kilda, sad that her father had been unable to come to see her pottery exhibition, saying she had been very ill, had lost 30 pounds and had spent all her money on doctors' bills. Could she go on a holiday? After receiving £20 from her father she thanked him and for 'his lovely letter, I'll be glad of your return from New Guinea'. She made a lot of her own clothes and reported on family matters such as Charles' son's illness (he'd had his adenoids out). She also thanked him for his gift of *The Mill on the Floss*.

In November 1939, Charles cabled his father with the good news that he had been appointed head appraiser for the New Zealand wool clip. A later letter from his wife Margaret thanked Hughes for the books he had sent her. On 9 October 1941, there was a note from Lily thanking her Dada for the money he had sent for her fence: 'I always think of you when the Japanese seem particularly menacing, you always recognised their menace to Australia ... Charles is a good brother to me', and again thanking him for the 'wee house'. A lady artist called Beth Lowe came to live with her. Charles continued through the 1940s to send regular letters to his father, updating him on the state of Lily's health, his fire-watching duties — roughly once a month — the state of the wool market, his golf, his wife's golf (very good) and the two children, usually concluding with the same words: 'As ever news is scarce your loving son Charles'.

Arthur's wife Mabel wrote to thank Hughes for his help in trying to reduce her husband's working hours. Arthur, she wrote, had aged a lot. One daughter, Gwen, had had a very bad time with the loss of her baby but was recovering.

The life political carries on

When Hughes was once more appointed as attorney-general, for the fourth time, as well as Minister for Industry in the new Lyons Government, Menzies wrote to congratulate him: 'Age cannot wither you nor custom stale your infinite variety'. One George Dash wrote, 'one quality which has shone undimmed throughout the whole of your distinguished career is your humbleness', recalling an occasion in 1917 when Hughes was at Helidon with his 'beloved colleagues Senator Tom Givens and the late Percy Deane' and quoted John Adamson's description of Hughes: 'loquacity, pugnacity, tenacity, and sagacity'. Best wishes came from an old school friend, S.H. Baxter, of Northbridge: 'The Fulham boy wishes the Chelsea boy every success. May he get in on the flood as he came originally.' Lyons died suddenly in April 1939 and Hughes became Deputy Leader, only just losing the leadership to Menzies, and was appointed Minister for Industry and later the Navy. Initially he had only been offered the Navy portfolio and sent a sharp note to Menzies saying that Industry was the appropriate job for him; the Navy was a non-job.

In December a letter came to him from a regular correspondent in London, more literate than most, commenting on the political scene in Britain at the time: 'The School tie and the Uncivil Service are the greatest dangers we have to our existence. Even Churchill is not immune to the continuous pressure of the old gang, wholly patriotic but so bloody out of date as to constitute a really definite danger. The best thing the Germans have done so far was to bomb the Carlton Club.' His comments on some of the leading British politicians of the day were pithy and not devoid of sense, though in the case of Attlee he was proved to have been way off mark: 'Lloyd George: an old 78, yellow haired, shrunken, trembling hands, out of touch with everything. Halifax: a parsonical bloke, high Church. Duff Cooper: first class snob, dictatorial. Put you in here for three months and send forth with flaming torch would be my choice.' And as for Labour, they were 'a poor mob: Bevan: big noise, talks big but does nothing outstanding. Attlee: hopeless, school tie, anaemic and looks it. Morrison: talks well, energetic, pushful.' Amery wrote as well, urging Hughes to get his 'people braced for German designs on New Guinea and Tanganyika'.

In the 1941 honours list Hughes was made a Companion of Honour (CH), and messages of congratulation flooded in from the likes of Sir Arthur Streeton, Tom Roberts, Major General Gordon Bennett, and a Dr Lovat who wrote: 'The one thing your enemies would like you to take (and which I know you won't ever take) is a knighthood. It lifts little men up and it pulls big men down),' and in Welsh from J. Gordon Jones: 'Llongyfarchiadau cynnes ar anrhydedd uchel rhoddwyd i chwi gan Brenin Lloegr.' On the original, Hughes, in his own handwriting, wrote over each word the English translation: 'Warm congratulations on the high honour bestowed upon you by England's King'. Some letters came addressed to the 'cloddiwr bach', Welsh for 'little digger', another from Canada quoting the old Welsh proverb 'Dyfal donc a dyrr y garreg', which a free translation would render as 'perseverance will out'.

The ALP won the 1941 election under the leadership of Curtin, and Hughes became leader of the United Australia Party, forging a close liaison with the Country Party and its leader Sir Arthur Fadden, who found Hughes a loyal colleague 'with no dictatorial tendencies'. Fadden in his book recorded an exchange between them: Fadden asked why Hughes hadn't joined the Country Party since he had been a member of all the other parties at one time or another, to which Hughes replied: 'I had to draw the line somewhere'. In September of the same year the *Daily Telegraph* asked their readers to write to the newspaper with the names of those they regarded as the most important Australians: Hughes was voted the greatest of the politicians. Commemorating his birthday later in the year, the Melbourne *Sun* wrote of him: 'He has never been respectful about party lines. He is a hard man to work with or for. He has terrified private secretaries, rocked cabinets, lashed oppositions. His hearing is dull but his tongue is sharp: Wizened and sardonic, a master of calculated indiscretion, a volcano that erupts when by all natural laws it should be extinct; a health then in these sour regimented days to a superb individualist, to a vital survival from a civilised past. There is only one Billy, parchment faced, courageous, exasperating, fascinating grand little man.'

Chapter 14

Grand old man

The following July, a grand dinner was held in Parliament House in his honour to celebrate his 50 years in the New South Wales and Federal Parliaments. One newspaper article called him 'an anachronism', saying that meeting him was 'like meeting Captain Arthur Sydney on Circular Quay'; another that the 'gnome-like shell' housed a man of amazing vitality for one of his age and he still took his morning gallop though his appearances on the golf course were more rare. He received a very handsome handwritten tribute from Curtin, saying 'much of what I am is your tilling'. At the dinner Curtin read a telegram from Arthur Mailey and Jim Bancks; the latter had said that he had created his character Ginger Meggs because he believed he was 'the lineal successor to you'.[1] Although an admirer of Curtin, who was often described as political enemy but personal friend, Hughes continually opposed what he saw as Labor slipping under the influence of the communists: 'The head of the coalminers federation is a communist, the general secretary of the Waterside Workers is a communist, the general secretary of the Iron Workers Union is a communist ... these are men who take their policy from the Communist Executive which in its turn takes its Directions from Moscow.'

He had also been an impish and occasional fierce critic of Curtin and Beazley's policy of isolationism and was still capable of 'brilliant invective, pungent analysis and spell binding emotionalism'. Although disparaging of the strutting nonsense of 'Il Duce', Hughes was opposed to Britain going to war over Abyssinia — 'midsummer madness' in his view — and he was content for Mussolini and Haile Selassie to 'stew in their own juices'. During the 1930s, however, he had become more and more concerned with the threat he saw posed by the increasing militarism of both Germany and Japan. Nevertheless, in April 1941, he accepted an invitation to a reception given by the Consul General of Japan at his residence at Point Piper in Sydney, which oddly had a Welsh name, 'Craig y Mor' ('Rock of the Sea'). He remained resolute in his belief that the aim of Japan was 'to enslave the world ... to make themselves the ruling caste over a world of fettered helots'. Newspapers were to write of him as being at that time almost alone among Australian statesmen in setting forth the dangers of Nazism and Fascism.

There was no doubt a bittersweet moment when the government introduced conscription: 'And Curtin who for twenty five years had denounced me for conscripting Australians for service overseas — which I never attempted to do — after pledging himself most solemnly not to introduce conscription — did so.' In his speech in Parliament on the bill to introduce conscription he expanded:

> Put shortly what the Prime Minister says is this. Conscription for overseas service which was not only unnecessary but a violation of the fundamental principles of individual liberty, and so an infamous and accursed thing has now become a patriotic duty ... For twenty seven years virulent opposition to conscription has been one of its [the ALP's] basic tenets. Although I have been held up to obloquy for a generation as the arch-priest of conscription, I did no more than to give the people an opportunity to say whether they would accept or reject conscription for overseas service ... [There has] always been something artificial about the anti-conscription cry ... It was a cry manufactured to camouflage deep-seated anti-empire, anti-British sentiment ... In the last war he [Curtin] was not only one of the most active in the anti-conscription campaign, but was a leading propagandist against Australia's participation in the war.

The speech, polemical and well-honed as ever, was entirely disingenuous: the situations pertaining in World War I and those confronting Australia in World War II were very different. In 1917, few Australians believed that their homeland was under threat of invasion, but with the

Grand old man

fall of Singapore the swift occupation by the Japanese of most of South East Asia and the Pacific Islands, Darwin having been bombed, and enemy submarines sighted in Sydney waters, the prospect of invasion was a real and present danger. British influence in the Far East had been much eroded over the years and Curtin rightly saw the US as Australia's most important defence ally — and this before General Macarthur established his command in Australia. The country obviously was in tune with Curtin's views and gave Labor a landslide victory in the August 1943 elections, with the opposition badly split between Fadden and Menzies, the United Australia Party reduced to 14 seats and the Country Party down to nine. The leadership passed to Menzies, with Hughes becoming Deputy Leader.

The 1944 election saw Hughes returned with a majority of 8588 and, as an indication of his continuing vitality at the age of 82, he made an arduous trip to the Northern Territory, visiting Alice Springs and the bombed Darwin, covering some 20 000 miles in 14 days. The trip was organised by the army and much enjoyed by Hughes: numerous photographs taken during his visit to attest to his evident bonhomie. That year also saw some of the worst bushfires that Victoria had ever suffered, with the destruction of 500 homes and thousands of miles of fencing, and the death of 1 million sheep, 50 000 cattle, 1000 horses, an equal number of pigs, and 200 000 poultry. The accompanying drought was as bad, so bad that farmers in mid-year were suffering almost as much as their colleagues who had lost their properties in the fires. 'Old man drought is on one of his worst benders', wrote Hughes.

Debate in Federal Parliament recorded that the drought in Victoria, New South Wales and South Australia ranked in severity with the droughts of 1902 and 1914. The cities simply didn't realise the effects of the drought in the bush: 'There are not so very many of us, even in a representative group such as this house who have lived on the land and experienced the rigours of drought'. Hughes spoke in Parliament in favour of ample compensation for those who had suffered, from whatever source, and had lost little of his capacity for memorable and telling metaphor. 'If a beggar or a starving man asks me for food I do not give him a coin or produce a sandwich with my visiting card bearing the inscription: Here is a sandwich from WM Hughes. Those who are in need are not interested in where the relief comes from.'

The year 1944 also saw him expelled from yet another party, this time for rejoining the War Council when his party had decided to leave it. Menzies had written to him on 18 February 1944 saying that he had no alternative but to resign from the War Council following the party's decision. Hughes sent his resignation the same day, as requested. However, Prime Minister Curtin was very loath to lose his services, and particularly the experience he had gained during World War I. He and Hughes then connived to get him reinstated. A private note from Curtin to Hughes requested him to reconsider his position and remain a member of the War Council. In a handwritten addition Curtin wrote: 'You can make what changes or additions you would like' to the suggested note. Hughes did so, rejoined the council, and out of the United Australia Party he went. When Curtin died in his sleep in July 1945 one of the warmest tributes to him in Parliament came from Hughes.

And when the war was over . . .

After the war he joined the Liberal Party but was never quite of it. The party had been formed from the wreckage of the United Australian Party, and Hughes was chosen as one of its New South Wales candidates in 1945. He had been opposed in the preselection process by a certain Turner who, according to a McNair survey at the time, was the clearly preferred candidate. After his departure from the Treasury bench he showed no sense of abating his interest in the political game. He was active in his constituency, took up cause after cause on behalf of his constituents, and patronised and supported a vast variety of societies and causes: Willoughby Homing Pigeon Society, Melbourne Savage Club, Surf Life Saving Association of Australia, North Shore Rowing Club. At the age of 85 he was still doing woodcarving, sending his requests for screws and nails to the managing director or owner. On one occasion he presented a jewel casket he had made to the wife of the licensee of the Canberra Hotel, where he always stayed.

One cause he pursued was the installation of a telephone kiosk in Palm Beach, his intervention with the Department of Posts and Telegraphs producing rapid action and fulsome praise from Hughes in a letter to the deputy director of the department: 'All hail, Thane of Cawdor and worker of miracles — thank you — a fair, a lovely CABINET standing slyly like a young maiden in some Arcadian Grove awaiting the coming of her lover ... like Aladdin I had rubbed the Magic Lamp and whispered in the ear of the Genie. And he had gone straight away and got the dashed thing. Wonderful and splendid.'

He made regular contributions to charities and worthy causes over the years: In 1946 donations went to:

> North Shore Adult Deaf and Dumb Association
> Northern Suburbs Rugby Union Club
> Retired Sailors Soldiers and Airmen
> Imperial League of Australia
> Boy Scouts and Girl Guides Association
> Children's Hospital
> Totally and Permanently Disabled Soldiers Association
> Salvation Army
> Smith Family
> Mater Misericordia Hospital

And, of course, he claimed tax relief on them all.

In July 1945, he visited Queensland as a member of the Commonwealth parliamentary delegation along with Mary and his masseur Bachli, who usually accompanied him on most trips. 'Masseur' was not a category of occupation recognised by the Public Service Board and in order to have his travel met from the public purse he was described as a ministerial messenger. Writing to Edward Hanlon, the Premier of Queensland, he said of Bachli: 'I have had him for donkeys years, a masseur of great potency; He is my man Friday, where I go, he goes.' His office kept him up to date with events in Canberra while he was away; one message included the question: 'who fathered the 40 hour week? Australian Congress of Trade Unions? No. The Government?

No. Robinson Crusoe, after all he got everything done by Friday.' During his visit a certain young man called Joh Bjelke-Petersen tried and failed to see him.

A star immortal

Relations with his family ran their normal course: in July 1944, Hughes had helped Charles get a priority permit to go on the train to Melbourne, and for Christmas that year had presented all the children (except Ethel) with lottery tickets. Christmas cards came from all the family, children, grandchildren, nieces and nephews and all were assiduously filed. The card from Lily included a poem she had composed:

> Out of time and space He came
> A Star immortal and a King.
> This earth was dark with sin profound
> Then Light Divine shone all around.
> Just for a little space of Time
> He dwelt upon this earthly clime
> And man was charmed by His Sweet Face
> And came for Balm and Heaven's Grace.
> Until sad hatred's bitter Force
> Prevailed to nail Him on a Cross:
> Ah Saddest yet most Blessed Day!
> No Pow'r can quench that Sacred Flame.
> But soaring high from Sin's Sad State
> The Star ascends to Heaven's Gate:
> Where He forever intercedes
> With God for Man's Immortal Needs

In November the following year Lily had fallen sick again: she had suffered a slight stroke and the expenses were heavy, eliciting £25 from Hughes to help defray the costs. Beth Lowe wrote in lieu of Lily since the stroke had affected her right hand, but wished to thank her father for the money. A similar letter came a month later noting that Lily would need help around the house. Often the letters were full of remarks about the garden and asking her father about his garden.

The year 1946 saw an improvement in Lily's condition, although the recovery was slow. Hughes arranged for the Commonwealth Bank to make a monthly payment of £15 to her 'until further notice'. Lily wrote herself to say that some power was returning to her arm. She sent her best wishes to Dolly, Bill and Arthur and included a telling sentence which showed the tensions that must have once existed between Mary and the children of the first family: 'Tell Mary I have forgotten the past and send regards.'

Margaret, Charles' wife, wrote on 6 May 1947 commiserating with her father-in-law on a fall he had had, reporting that Charles had not been well and had almost had a breakdown but was picking up; and adding that Bill and Margaret were doing well, with young Bill later working for British and Dominion Traders. For Christmas 1948, the children received cheques for £5 from their father, Lily sending thanks and saying her garden was ablaze with roses, poppies, delphiniums, lobelias, hollyhocks, carnations and snapdragons. Three months later Charles wrote to congratulate his father on having been selected for the new constituency in North Sydney; Dolly reported that she had acquired a chinchilla cat: 'pure white with deep golden eyes'.

Having sat at various times for three different constituencies — West Sydney 1901–17, Bendigo 1917–22, North Sydney 1922–49 — Hughes moved to the new seat of Bradfield in 1949, his supporters fearing that he might have lost the North Sydney seat as a result of redistribution. He still took on numerous speaking engagements on behalf of other Liberal candidates, as well as campaigning on his own behalf. He won the election and messages of congratulation came in waves from Menzies, Page, Richard Casey, Enid Lyons, Larry Anthony, 'Black Jack' McEwen, Bill McMahon, Artie Fadden, Percy Spender and, perhaps incongruously, a Sister Coupe from the Maternity Hospital, Albany. A visitor to Hughes' office in Parliament following his re-election remarked on its somewhat Spartan appearance, the sole decorations being a bust of Churchill and on the wall an Arab proverb: 'I had no shoes and I complained, until I saw a man who had no feet.'

Billy Hughes

He liked McEwen and, according to Enid Lyons, once said to her of him, 'He says in twenty words what you and I would say in two ... Ah there you are, he's just gone over the whole of the dairy herds of New South Wales not merely cow by cow but teat by teat'. The *Herald* wrote of Hughes' election: 'Although at 84 [he was actually 87 in 1949] he has lost much of his ancient fire, Mr Hughes remains a dominating figure — the only member of the opposition to whom the Labor benches pay the tribute of hushed and respectful silence.' In an interview with him in the same year, *The Times* (Sydney) noted that he could read the smallest print without glasses, and had very supple limbs (which is somewhat at variance with the recollection of closer acquaintances that he had to be practically unscrambled in the mornings, limb by limb, but perhaps it reflected on the efficacy of Bachli's ministrations). He was also reported as being able to open a car door with his toes. The day after the election of 10 December he wrote in his engagement book: 'Breathe freely, Eat Sleep, Rest DV.'

Who boundless is ...

In July 1950, Mary Gilmore wrote to him regarding her wish to donate a tray with a painting on it to the National Gallery; it was in her view a very special painting, the first example of Aboriginal art painted on plastic. She also included 'my last not very good piece of verse', which strangely encapsulated much of what she saw in Hughes, whether intentionally or not:

> Again, where at low tide the rocks emerge
> As the slow tumble of the seas asperge
> As long ago I watch across the dim
> The moonglades on the far horizon's rim
> Adventure calls and with incessant urge
> Beats these bent shoulders with its living scourge.
> Maybe the Cherubim and Seraphim
> As with veiled faces bowed they worship Him
> Who boundless is, are but man's inward cry
> To break the bondage of this narrow verge

And in the endless vast of time to swim
Ageless, unbroken, where Nirvanas lie.
And yet, man more than the mollusc is
Adventure even as death, is his.

His last election came in 1951. After an attempt to make him undergo preselection there was an outcry which made party officials back off and eat humble pie when he was selected unopposed and — after the double dissolution of Parliament and despite being described as a 'bag of bones held together by his veins' — won the election of 28 April with a majority of 22 881. In September the New South Wales Chamber of Manufacturers held a splendid dinner to honour him on his 87th (actually his 89th) birthday. He prepared the speech with his usual care and was reported in the press admonishing his audience to be ever on their guard against the threat of communism and potential territorial designs of Japan.

An eclectic mind

Hughes exemplified the axiom that longevity, apart from the accident of good health and inherited genes, owes much to maintaining a keen sense of curiosity. Throughout his life, undiminished by the weight of years, he remained unfailingly curious, exhibiting an eclectic interest in a sometimes bewildering array of subjects. By choice and fortunate accident he was involved in some of the major developments of the twentieth century from the perspective of Australia: the development of aviation and radio, the Snowy Mountains Scheme, the opening up of New Guinea, the search for minerals and, later, the development of nuclear energy. In addition to curiosity he had a persistent optimism and faith in the future: there was always a silver lining to be found beyond the darkest cloud. His favourite remark on the state of the world was that 'things were getting better all the time'.

Not only was he punctilious in acquiring supporting material for his parliamentary speeches, he kept snippets of sometimes esoteric memorabilia, such as decorative examples of orations made by him or in his honour, or formal addresses when given the freedom of cities in the UK. He noted a gift of Brownell Tasmanian potatoes from the Commonwealth potato controller and a brace of pheasants and a leash of partridges received for Christmas. Time and time again he pursued the Government statistician and Parliamentary Library with detailed demands for information, be it views on creating a Jewish settlement in the Kimberleys, or inventions by Australians (a list of which he kept for speeches, which included Aeroplane: Lawrence Hargrave; Refrigeration: I.S. Mort; Torpedo: Louis Brennan in Melbourne in 1887; Automatic Totalisator: Sir George Julius).

Another of his more abiding interests was aviation. Imperial Airways wrote to him April 1931, for example, stating 'This letter is coming to you by the first Air Mail from England to Australia covering in fifteen days'. He had taken a keen interest in aviation from its earliest days and was always a supporter of extending Australia's embryonic air travel. In a letter dated 30 January 1947 he replied rather crossly to Qantas (or 'Quantas' as he wrongly spelled it), which had asked him to verify whether it had been Bruce who had been the first PM to travel on business by air; 'The facts are', he replied, 'that I was PM 1915–1923. In 1916 I attended the war Cabinet in London and was absent from Australia for some 7 to 8 months. On two occasions over to France to visit the AIF. I inaugurated the first flight from England to Australia offering £10 000 pounds for the first plane making the journey under 30 days ... Ross and Keith Smith won.'

This episode had in fact much rankled Bert Hinkler, one of Australia's other intrepid aviators, who did as much as anyone to combat the 'tyranny of distance'. Hinkler believed that he had been cheated out of participating in the race by the imposition of unfair conditions and blamed Hughes, 'with his big wide, Welsh, noisy mouth'.[2] Noisy it may have been but the few recordings of him in his later years betray a rather mellifluous voice, not rasping, and without an Australian, Cockney or Welsh accent. The *Sun Pictorial* once wrote that he had a 'sweet tenor voice' and one writer remembered him singing 'The Moon Behind the Hill'. In 1918 it was Hughes who broadcast the first direct radio message from the UK (from Caernarfon in Wales) to Australia (received at Wahroonga in Sydney), at least according to traditional accounts. However, Colin Mackinnon, writing in the H.R.S.A. Radio Waves, showed that in actual fact the first message was from Joseph Cook, Minister for the Navy: 'Oh dear we can't have the Navy Minister taking precedence over the Prime Minister'.

Hughes had also been a dominating figure in the development of the Commonwealth Scientific and Industrial Research Organisation (CSIRO). Sir George Currie, who wrote of the origins of the CSIRO, remarked that 'Hughes was years — 50 years ahead of his time' with his objective to launch a national research fund and coordinate the work of different research agencies and universities. Hughes wanted scientists to be 'if not the captains, then the pilots of industry'. The British Government had published a white paper on a 'Scheme for the Organisation and Development of Scientific and Industrial Research' which impressed Hughes and he discussed it with the then Minister of Works in Victoria, F.W. Hagelthorn, who he knew reasonably well. A lunch was organised by the University of Melbourne with the intention of progressing the idea of establishing an Australian equivalent. In attendance were the premiers of Victoria, New South Wales and South Australia, and of course Hughes, who to the astonishment and no doubt delight of his co-diners announced that the government was in favour of the idea and would commit £500 000 to its development. In 1916, the Hughes Government established the Advisory Council of Science and Industry with the aim of developing it into a National Laboratory. This was followed by an act to set up the Commonwealth Institute of Science and Technology, passed by the Australian Parliament in 1920. It was not until 1946 that it acquired its present appellation.

Another abiding interest was Australia's unforgiving climate. Scattered through his papers are notes and cuttings concerning the climate, especially the impact of drought and the issue of water supply. Many papers referred to the drought in Queensland in 1926 that had resulted in the loss of so much livestock and which, according to Hughes, had been so bad that the frogs had 'forgotten how to swim'. The problem was, he felt, that nature could not be changed; some parts of the country were getting too much rain, some too little, and what was necessary was to get the water from the one to the other. He was in favour of the Bradfield Scheme,[3] taking the flood water of the rivers in the coastal mountains of North Queensland and using them for irrigation and power, and also storing rainfall in the McDonnell and Musgrave Ranges. In a similar vein, in 1944 he induced a full report from the government on the disastrous drought and fires in the ACT and New South Wales when Broken Hill was 'within cooee of disaster'. He was to remain passionately interested in this and all such ideas of import to Australia — and the world — until very near his death.

Chapter 15

The peaceful aftermath

The records of Billy Hughes' last years were little different from those he kept before, only now there were more rememberances of things past, and his correspondence was composed more of letters from nephews and nieces, grandsons and granddaughters. People still wrote from Wales and ex-servicemen still sought favours, but the fascinating thing is that they kept on coming. What was the magic of this old, old man (by anyone's definition) that commanded such interest and even reverence and made them wish to be in contact with him? Letter writing of course was a universal practice among literate men and women, and Hughes had been in the political game for longer than anyone else at a time when politicians still enjoyed huge respect; furthermore, whatever the outbursts of his youth and crustiness of his old age, maybe the magnetism of the legend still pulsated softly for a newer generation?

An old man remembers

The tenor of his later papers partly suggests veneration for old age, but also intimates that in his later years Hughes' hard edges had been sandpapered down, revealing a softer persona under the crabby shell. Among this miscellany was an article from a *Sunday Mirror* of 1960, quoting Frank Green, Clerk of the House of Representatives from 1937 to 1955, who wrote: 'kindly affection for him in his old age was a sort of amused affection one might feel for a pet cheetah, from which no affection could be expected in return'. Hughes kept a letter from an ex-Lieutenant Arnold of the Royal Dublin Fusilliers; it contained a report of Hughes' nephew Captain Brian Hughes, who had been killed in action by grenade concussion at the last gasp of the war while attempting to take a copse where the 'Bosch' had a machine gun post; touchingly it said, 'There was not a mark upon him'. Frank sent congratulations on his birthday from Perth and hoped he was taking his vitamin C. Nieces from various branches of the family wrote affectionate letters: Florrie Collins said 'Dear Uncle, Bill looks very much like his mother', Winifred Whitney wrote from Chorley, Lancashire; and Maggie Hughes Gaskell sent birthday greetings. There is a letter from one Rachel Jenkins, the daughter of Hughes' cousin Elizabeth Price of Hirwaun in South Wales; Rachel's son, she added, was a seaman on HMS *Illustrious*. Hughes even wrote a memo to himself to buy *Teach Yourself Greek*.

In 1951, in his 89th year, he was still inserting details into his diary for possible use in speeches or parliamentary questions. Again it was a miscellany — of wool statistics ('The Australian wool cheque for 1950–51 reached a record £636 330 574 from the sale of 3 547 195 bales …'); population statistics; industrial statistics ('Terms of Oil Agreement 1921–2'); and international data (e.g. 'Russia's Armed Forces'). As peppery as ever, when asked to give the vote of thanks to a Government Minister, Doug Anthony, instead of the usual platitudes Hughes launched an attack on the unsuspecting Minister for the delays in providing telephones in Hughes' electorate — Anthony being Postmaster General. The Minister was not amused, though the audience was delighted. Hughes too, enjoyed other 'enfants terribles' who were not unabashed to prick the balloons of pompous parliamentarians.

A resplendent dinner was held at Parliament House on 25 September to honour him on his 88th birthday, actually his 90th. He recorded the speech he was to make and, on hearing the tape, remarked: 'If that really is me then the modern scientist can make a little man like me sound like a cross between a revolt in a madhouse and a whooping cough epidemic in a fever ward.' In the speech his wit was still evident: 'Although it is not in my present intention to spend the next 58 years in Parliament, one can never tell what one can do if one is goaded to it.'

He also repeated what he had once written to his friend Ben Tillett at Transport House London: 'I came into politics to fight for the underdog. And I have done so for 58 and a half years.' Speaking to journalists afterwards he remarked, to nobody's surprise, 'I have not spent my public life in meek submission to those who sought to pull me from my perch', and with a large tongue in cheek praised Australians for their perspicacity in regularly returning him to office: 'they might go to the dogs and bet on ponies but they had enough sense to keep me in Parliament.'

Just a month before his death the Sydney Sanitorium and hospital wrote to him concerning Miss Edith Haynes, Mary's niece, and daughter of a one-time editor of *The Bulletin*. Edith had lived as a companion with the Hughes for many years at Lindfield and was looked after generously, with Hughes paying exceptional costs incurred by her, such as hospital fees when she entered Prince Alfred Hospital at Camperdown, Sydney, with breast cancer. He had also helped her to get a job with the Attorney General's office at Circular Quay in 1925 at a salary of £198 per annum. The hospital wrote that Edith was suffering from 'an anxiety state'. Hughes replied: 'What she needs is treatment that will distract her mind from the mental and help her to help herself. This is a very beautiful world and we are among the most fortunate people in it ... Please let me have your weekly account.' He was obviously very fond of her and to an extent she had partly filled the void left by Helen's death. When Hughes died, Mary sold the Lindfield house and bought a unit at Darling Point where she and Edith lived together until Mary's death in 1958.

When he fell ill in October 1952, shortly after being honoured with a Doctorate of Law by Sydney University, there were innumerable letters sent to his home wishing him a rapid recovery, many from old diggers: several looked forward to the next billiard game with Hughes, while one referred to his usual spot in Martin Place, in the centre of Sydney, for the annual Anzac Day parade (for years after his death an empty chair was placed on the spot for the parade, with the digger's khaki slouch hat on the seat). The *Auckland Herald* wrote that he was recovering and that his first request had been for a cup of tea, a ginger ale and the newspapers. The BBC broadcast a report of his progress on 16 October 1952. A week before his death Hughes received a letter saying, 'Your daughter [Dolly] asked to write and say how sorry she was not to have been able to write to you during your illness'; she was in fact in the Alfred Hospital in Melbourne — in the family she had the reputation of being rather fey and 'towards the end, lost the plot'.

A few days before his death his doctor reported that he had become most upset at cabled reports that Welsh Nationalists were seeking home rule and had attempted to sabotage the Queen's visit to Wales. A day before his death a letter arrived from Tudor Glyn Hughes, a cousin, to report that his father had died: 'one of the last links with your boyhood days'; his cousin added that he'd found several of Hughes' letters to his father in 1917 — Hughes scribbled on the letter, 'card sent'.

Billy Hughes died peacefully, in his sleep, on 28 October 1952. His last words were to the caretaker of his house, Ron Amunsden: 'Tell Mary to go to bed and not to worry.' Amunsden was to boast that he held a record: of never having been sacked by Hughes (who, he said, had been a good employer). Hughes' doctor, Lyall Ducker, who had seen him a few hours before his death, said that basically Hughes had died of exhaustion. Lily wrote to Dame Mary after her father's death to thank her for the photographs Mary had sent her of her father. She liked the one showing him getting his honorary degree. Lily said she had lost the sight of one eye and that the delphiniums were lovely: 'Dad always loved to see things growing didn't he?' Margaret also wrote Mary a letter of condolence and she, too, referred to the degree ceremony as well as the delightful two days spent with them in Canberra and at Lindfield.

Last respects

The funeral saw one of the biggest crowds Sydney had ever seen and St Andrews Cathedral in Sydney full to the brim. His son Bill was one of the pallbearers, though Charles was unable to be present. Three old diggers wearing proudly the badge of the Totally and Permanently

Incapacitated Soldiers Association squeezed in with difficulty, one being heard to remark: 'I didn't agree with his politics but I'll not hear a word against him.' A little boy of five carried some bedraggled roses to the chancel step in front of the altar: his father said, to no-one in particular, 'I've come down from Bathurst, he got my Dad a pension 30 years ago and he helped me too in 1946'. People of all ages and all persuasions, both political and religious, attended. Apart from the expected eulogies there were some more than normally interesting features, particularly the speech by the Lord Archbishop of Sydney and Primate of Australia, who referred to Hughes' great love of the Chinese, astonishing them with his knowledge of their ancient classics (the President of the Chinese Chamber of Commerce, Mr Henry Lan Yip, had been a frequent visitor to Enderslie). The Jewish people in Australia likewise had lost a good friend in Hughes, and the Mater Misericordia Hospital lamented the loss of their good friend.

While he did (intermittently) attend church, religion as such seemed not to have impinged too greatly on his preoccupations: 'I am a Christian', he said and, 'Christians believe in repentance'. Commenting on an alleged faith healer he remarked that 'one can't be a Christian and not believe that these things are possible'. Speaking at a Salvation Army meeting he once said, 'Men cannot find God through a formula nor be brought to accept the teaching of Christ by logic. The new order if it is to endure must begin in our hearts and the Christian religion teaches us how men may live in peace and happiness all the days of their lives.' He believed that his 'role was that of the political Christian, one who returned good for evil'. On another occasion he said it was 'impossible to imagine a rational explanation for the development of life on this planet ... think of the miracle of life, evolution may explain a lot but it cannot explain all'. He was buried in the Northern Suburbs Cemetery alongside his daughter Helen.

The *Sunday Herald* lauded his vision and astonishing record, his devotion to the cause of Australia, and his vigilance to the last to safeguard the land he loved, but with rare objectivity also wrote: 'How much greater he would have been as a statesman ... if he had not suffered from the defects of his dazzling qualities — if coolness of judgement and temperament had gone with his unrivalled powers but then — he would not have been Billy Hughes.' As people had said often, he had become a legend in his own lifetime, but they might have added that the legend was no greater than the reality.

Mary Gilmore wrote:

> Now let all meanness die
> And envy hide its head
> This is the hour of loss
> In which we mourn the dead
> Although with whiplash tongue
> He turned an asp irate
> He stood above the ruck
> Where small men breed their hate
> Let the slow tread of feet
> March where the deep drums beat
> Let the sad hearts of all
> That saddest sound repeat
> He was a beacon light
> He dared the leader's path
> His were the storms and our
> The peaceful aftermath.

Letters and telegrams of condolence in their hundreds came to Lady Mary and were all filed assiduously. They came from people of all walks and stations of life, literally from pauper and king. One even came from Patrick Mathew Brosnan, who had thrown the fateful egg at him that day at Warwick: 'Billy was a great old feller. I would have loved to meet him but never did. I hit him fair and square on the mouth as he arrived at the Warwick railway station.' McCristal, who had so abused him in his book and engineered his dismissal from the Sydney branch of the Wharfies Union, spoke well of him and his contribution to the cause of the working man, despite their disagreement over conscription.

All strings tied

An early handwritten draft of Hughes' will, dated 23 May 1930, made the following provisions in the event of his death:

> 3000 ... Bill (Ernest Morris)
>
> 3000 ... Charlie (Charles Leonard)
>
> 1000 ... Ethel
>
> 1000 ... Lily
>
> 1000 ... Dorothy
>
> To my step-son Arthur Clifford Hughes ... 1000
>
> 500 ... Shirley Deane (Daughter of Percy Deane)
>
> 500 ... George Payne 28 Coverton Rd. Tooting
>
> To Mary ... House Lindfield + 2/3rds of the income from the residue of the estate, the remainder to Helen, also Sassafras + the land there and 1/3rd of the estate provided she reaches 21 or until Mary's decease.

His last will followed the broad lines of the 1930 draft but took account of Helen's death and that of George Payne. Shirley Deane was omitted and Mary's niece Edith inserted. The main provisions of the will stipulated that all plate, of whatever description, was to be divided equally between his two sons and Edith, and one-third of his real and personal property up to £5000 was to go to the three girls, with any sum in excess to be divided equally between his sons, stepson and Edith. If the various dispositions in the will had been met, any residual amount was to be paid to the Burnside Presbyterian Orphan Homes, Parramatta, to be used for the erection and maintenance of a home to be known as 'The William Morris Hughes Home'. The will was finalised and witnessed on 16 September 1937.

From the content of the will it is clear that at that stage the house at Sassafras had not been sold. In a letter from Mulligan to the chief librarian of the Mitchell Library, with photographs of the unveiling of the plaque to Hughes in the crypt of St Pauls, he wrote that Hughes' estate was valued at £72 000, from which was deducted federal and state death duties amounting to £28 000: 'much more than I'll receive as solicitor for the Executor of this estate'. (Mulligan did, however, became chairman of directors of the Australian Italia Shipping Company and consul general for Costa Rica.) The affidavit of the executor, the Perpetual Trustee Company, shows that £26 710.3.0 was the property value of the house in Sydney, and in Victoria the personal estate was worth £45 758 15s 8d.

On 23 May 1938, Hughes had added a codicil: 'I direct that the maintenance and education of David Evan Hughes — now 9 months old — and under the guardianship of K.C. Duffy of Australia House London shall be a charge on my wife's estate under this will — or if she should predecease me — I direct that 5000 pounds be set aside from my estate for that purpose and that upon his attaining the age of 21 years the residuum, if any — should be paid to him, for his sole use and benefit.' The birth certificate of David Evan Hughes shows that he was born in Willesden at the Brondesbury Park address, the son of Helen Hughes, on 31 July 1937. The column in the birth certificate to note the father's name is blank. In Dame Mary's will the bulk of the £25 947 she left went to Edith Haynes, but intriguingly £3500 was left to David Evan Duffy and £1000 to Vincent Cyril Duffy. This Vincent Duffy, one must conclude, was the official named in Hughes' codicil (though it mentions 'K.C.' not 'V.C.' Duffy) as acting secretary at the Australian High Commission responsible for returning Helen's body to Australia and as the baby's guardian a year after his birth. An ABC dramatised version of Helen's tragic demise showed that her son, David, was alive in 2004 and living in Sydney, and had readopted his birth name of Hughes.

On 21 September 1955, Dame Mary auctioned much memorabilia, furniture and fittings from the Lindfield house, including many of her late husband's handcrafted objets d'art, coloured prints of King George V1 and the Mona Lisa, silver jugs, hundreds of books, the tea set Parliament had given them as a wedding present, a tray presented to Hughes by the Waterside Workers Federation, records and copies of Welsh songs.

The peaceful aftermath

In the half-century since his death the regular references to him in so many different contexts would not only have further titillated his abundant vanity but would no doubt have elicited a mordant 'Quite right too', leaving the listener in some uncertainty whether it was fully meant or not. When asked on one occasion to pose for a photograph he had said: 'I'm no prima donna. This publicity is like blowing up a frog — its funny for the people blowing but it's not funny for the frog.' He might also have thought that it was entirely appropriate that the last vote he cast in Parliament was with the Labor Party he had helped to establish, crossing the floor to vote against the government on its proposal to sell shares in Commonwealth Oil Refineries Ltd that he had founded. He would also have been delighted to learn that he was the maternal uncle of the Welsh mother of Mrs Mubarak, wife of the Egyptian president.[1]

His last written work, composed on his death-bed, was an article for the 25th anniversary of *Graya*, the journal of Grays Inn where he had been elected a bencher in May 1916. The final, strangely piquant entry he wrote in his diary was a quotation from *Hamlet*:

> What a piece of work is man, how noble in reason, how infinite in faculty, in form and moving how express and admirable, in action how like an angel, in apprehension how like a God, the beauty of the world, the paragon of councils. And yet to me what is this quintessence of dust. Man delights not me no, nor woman willed though by your smiling you seem to say so.

Notes

INTRODUCTION
SWAGMAN TO STATESMAN

1 These points were raised in personal discussion with the author.
2 Owen, *The Tempestuous Journey*.
3 Fitzhardinge, *That Fiery Particle* and *The Little Digger*.
4 Horne, *In Search of Billy Hughes* and *The Little Digger*.
5 Farmer Whyte, *William Morris Hughes*.
6 Manning Clark, 'One Year in the Life of William Morris Hughes', speech delivered at La Trobe University, 28 July 1982.
7 The recollection was included in Fadden's *They Call Me Artie*. Fadden became PM for 40 days in 1941 after Menzies' resignation, and was once taught the words of 'Botany Bay' by Hughes.
8 *Herald*, 28 October 1952.
9 Fadden, *They Call Me Artie*.

CHAPTER 1
THE EARLY YEARS

1 *L'information*, 20 April 1919.
2 Lord Riddell's 'Intimate Diary of the Peace Conference and After'. He was the official representative of the London and Provincial Newspapers to the Peace Conference.
3 National Library of Australia newspaper cutting, possibly from the *Liverpool Morning Post*. The cutting also contains a photograph of the house and the school.
4 No 52872, issued on 22 August 1921.
5 In 1965, a Gilbert Forbes wrote to the National Library of Australia describing the house as having a basement, ground floor, two storeys and a garden at the rear. He

explained he was writing to inform the librarian that the house was in an area due for redevelopment and might be pulled down. The librarian minuted the Prime Minister's office that they might wish to put a plaque on the house recording Hughes' residence there. The suggestion elicited an NFA ('no further action') and it was not until 13 December 1990 that a blue plaque to that effect was formally unveiled by the then Australian High Commissioner to the United Kingdom, Doug McClelland. A previous plaque to Hughes' memory was unveiled in the crypt of St Paul's on 15 October 1953 by the Duke of Gloucester a year after Hughes' death.

6   *Sun Herald*, 3 December 1961.

Chapter 2
First brushes with the bush

1   Fred Payne eventually obtained a regular job in Scotts Hotel, Collins Street, Melbourne. George Payne's son and daughter also emigrated to Australia some years later.
2   Hughes, *Policies and Potentates*.
3   Sladen, *From Boundary Rider to Prime Minister*.
4   Farmer Whyte, *William Morris Hughes*.
5   Garran, *Prosper the Commonwealth*.
6   Browne, *They Called Him Billy*.
7   The Rev. Charles Lundy was typical of many of Hughes admirers writing in an unpublished memoir circa 1978 of Hughes' golden voice. Lundy also wrote in the family Bible that he agreed with Hughes' view of Menzies as 'A prince in the aristocracy of bastards'.

Chapter 3
Family strife and political life

1   Evatt, *William Holman*.

Chapter 4
'Billy Bach' — the little Welshman

1   This is from a speech made in Sydney in 1947.
2   Quoted in Keith Murdoch's *War Speeches of Billy Hughes*. Murdoch arranged Hughes' speeches for publication after the war and obtained the serialisation rights for Hughes' book *The Splendid Adventure* for the *Melbourne Herald* for a fee of £500.

Notes

CHAPTER 5
THE SLIPPERY SLOPE

1 Quoted by Keith Murdoch in *War Speeches of Billy Hughes*.

CHAPTER 6
ROOM AT THE TOP

1 *Sydney Morning Herald*. Stockbroker and industrialist W.S. Robinson was born in Melbourne in 1876, and was at one time a financial writer for *The Age*.

2 The respective contributions in terms of manpower for the war from the Dominions were:
New Zealand 19.35%
Australia 13.43%
Canada 13.48%

3 Keith Murdoch, later Sir Keith, was born in 1885 and had been sent to Britain in 1908 partly for elocution lessons to cure his stammer. He attended the London School of Economics from 1908 to 1910, returned to *The Age* and in 1912 became political correspondent for the *Sydney Evening Sun*.

4 Riddell was at one time editor of *The News of the World*. This report comes from his war diary.

5 Lyons, *Among the Carrion Crows*.

CHAPTER 7
CONSCRIPTION AND THE BIRTH OF NATIONALISM

1 Both, for different reasons, had grown increasingly alarmed at the rising use of contraceptive devices and the need to encourage population growth. 'Populate or perish' became an historic political slogan ('copulate or perish' in the corridors of the Parliament). Mannix sent him a birthday telegram a month before Hughes' death: 'Warmest congratulations. You and I are becoming increasingly like the boy that stood on the burning deck.' Hughes maintained a continuing interest in Ireland from his experiences in the war cabinet and subsequently in the context of the Republic's push for home rule. While still prime minister he wrote: 'Ireland, although she's got home rule seems very disturbed and until they get rid of De Valera I do not think things will be much better'. Mary, however, was quite impressed on meeting the Irish leader and thought him most charming.

2   Holman in his unpublished book, *Six Years of Labor Government.*
3   Corrigan, *Mud, Blood and Poppycock.* Corrigan is a retired British Army General.
4   Duncan Hall letters, Mitchell Library Sydney.
5   Fowler, *Statesman or Mountebank.* The subject of this book was George Reid.
6   Raymond, *Uncensored Celebrities.*
7   Corrigan, *Mud, Blood and Poppycock.*
8   Holman in his unpublished book, *Six Years of Labor Government.*

Chapter 8
The Peace Conference

1   Charles Evan Hughes became Governor of New York in 1906, defeating William Randolph Hearst. He also became a member of the US Supreme Court in 1910, and Chief Justice in 1930. His view of war was that 'it should be made a crime and those who instigate it should be punished as criminals'.

Chapter 10
The frustrating years

1   Licence No 140099, issued 27 October 1924.
2   Lloyd's story was indeed interesting. He came to Blackstone and was helped by the community to open a shop, which expanded such that he was selling everything from drapery to ironmongery. After some years his health began to deteriorate and he was advised to move to the countryside. He went to a property in Wanora and began to cultivate a garden. He arranged an elaborate system of wires to enable him to get around the plot without damaging the plants, learnt how to prune and graft, bud fruit trees and grow grapes. Eventually he had an orchard of some 400 trees. Suffering depredations from the local fauna such as bandicoots and wallabies, Owen fenced his land, having the trees cut by friends, but sawing and splitting the wood with his own hands. After some five years he had around 210 acres under cultivation when the big flood struck in 1893. Neighbours a mile away were forced to flee the rising waters and were given refuge by Owen. They, the Vidoronis, had two daughters and all were cut off for many days. When they returned to their property everything had been swept away, so they stayed with Owen until their house could be rebuilt. The next year Owen married Edith the elder of the two Vidoroni daughters – the best bargain he maintained he had ever made. He wrote poetry, mainly in Welsh, and claimed to be a first cousin of Lloyd George. On his 93rd birthday he began the celebration by singing 'Hen Wlad fy Nhadau' ('Land of My Fathers'), the Welsh national anthem.
3   The ABC program was called 'Political Triptych'.

CHAPTER 11
FAMILIAL CONCERNS

1   Lloyd, *Parliament and the Press*.
2   From a letter of August 1929.

CHAPTER 13
HELEN — A SHADOW FELL

1   Letter to the *Sunday Sun*.
2   Langmore, *Prime Ministers' Wives*.
3   Browne, *They Called Him Billy*.

CHAPTER 14
GRAND OLD MAN

1   Ginger Meggs was (and is) an Australian cartoon character, a cheeky urchin who never grows up.
2   Mandle, *Going it Alone*.
3   Builder of the Sydney Harbour Bridge.

CHAPTER 15
THE PEACEFUL AFTERMATH

1   *The Australian*, 5 February 1982.

Bibliography

Books

Booker, Malcolm (1980) *The Great Professional: A Study of W. M. Hughes*, McGraw-Hill.

Browne, Frank (1946) *They Called Him Billy*, Sydney: Peter Hudson.

Corrigan, Gordon (2003) *Mud, Blood and Poppycock*, Orion.

Cwrt Mawr MS 678B National Library of Wales.

Daly, Fred (1984) *From Curtin to Hawke*, Melbourne: Sun Books.

Dunn, Michael (1984) *Australia and the Empire: From 1788 to the Present*, Fontana/Collins.

Evatt, Herbert Vere (1979) *William Holman: Australian Labour Leader*, Sydney: Angus & Robertson.

Fadden, Arthur W. (1969) *They Call Me Artie: The Memoirs of Sir Arthur Fadden*, Brisbane: Jacaranda Press.

Farmer Whyte, William (1957) *William Morris Hughes, His Life and Times*, Sydney: Angus & Robertson.

Fitzhardinge, Lawrence F. (1964) *William Morris Highes: A Political Biography, Vol. 1: That Fiery Particle 1862–1914*, Sydney: Angus & Robertson.

Fitzhardinge, Lawrence F. *William Morris Hughes: A Political Biography, Vol. 2: The Little Digger 1914–1952*, Sydney: Angus & Robertson.

Fowler, J.M. *Statesman or Mountebank: An Australian War Study*.

Garran, Robert (1958) *Prosper the Commonwealth*, Sydney: Angus & Robertson.

Horne, Donald R. (1979) *In Search of Billy Hughes*, Melbourne: Macmillan.

Horne, Donald R. (1983) *The Little Digger: A Biography of Billy Hughes*, Melbourne: Macmillan.

Hudson, W.J. (1978) *Billy Hughes in Paris: The Birthplace of Australian Diplomacy*, Melbourne: Thomas Nelson.

Hughes, William Morris (1910) *The Case for Labour*.

Hughes, William Morris (1929), *The Splendid Adventure*, London.

Hughes, William M. (1950) *Crusts and Crusades: Tales of Bygone Days*, Sydney: Angus & Robertson.

Hughes, William Morris (1950) *Policies and Potentates*, Angus and Robertson.

La Nauze, John Andrew (1979) *Alfred Deakin: A Biography*, Sydney: Angus & Robertson.

Langmore, Diane (1992) *Prime Ministers' Wives*, McPhee Gribble.

Lloyd, C.J. (1988) *Parliament and the Press*, Melbourne University Press.

Lord Riddell's Intimate Diary of the Peace Conference and After, (He was the official representative of the London and Provincial Newspapers to the Peace Conference).

Lyons, Enid (1972) *Among The Carrion Crows*, Rigby.

Mandle, W.F. (1980) *Going it Alone*, Penguin.

McCristal, T.W. (1922) *Sensational Exposure of W.M. Hughes, PC: Prime Minister of Australia: The Windsor Eviction*, Sydney: T.W. McCristal.

Morgan, J. Vyrnwy (1916) *The War and Wales*, Chapman and Hall.

Murdoch, Keith (ed.) *War Speeches of Billy Hughes*, Cassell.

Murphy, D.J. (1990) *TJ Ryan: A Political Biography*, UQP.

Nauge, J.A. *Alfred Deakin*.

Owen, Frank (1954) *Tempestuous Journey, Lloyd George, His Life and Times*, London: Hutchinson.

Raymond, E.T. (1918) *Uncensored Celebrities*, T.F. Unwin.

Sladen, D.B.W. (1916) *From Boundary Rider to Prime Minister*, London.

Souter, Gavin (1976) *Lion and Kangaroo: Australia 1901–1919, The Rise of a Nation*, Sydney: William Collins.

Spartalis, Peter (1983) *The Diplomatic Battles of Billy Hughes*, Melbourne: Hale & Iremonger.

Sprigg, Stanhope W. (1916) *WM Hughes: The Strong Man of Australia*, London: Arthur Pearson Ltd.

Newspapers

Liverpool Daily Post
Melbourne *Argus*
Melbourne *Punch*
Melbourne *Herald and Weekly Times*
The Times of London
The Bulletin
The Canberra Times
The Sydney Morning Herald
L'information
Daily Telegraph
The Sun

Index

Adamson, John 139
Amery, Leo 37, 38, 101, 124, 139
Amunsden, Ron 156
Anstey, Frank xiv, 29
Anthony, Doug 154
Anthony, Larry 147
Appleton, W.A. 22
Arnold, Matthew 7
Asquith, Herbert 41, 54, 64, 102
Attlee, Clement 139
Austen, Frank 47
Australia Party 120
Australian Democratic Front 50
Australian Expeditionary Force 55
Australian Imperial Force 54, 58, 59
Australian Labor Party ix, 22, 23, 28, 29, 31, 43, 63, 64, 68, 69–70, 74, 117, 119, 122, 125, 140, 141, 148, 161
Australian Workers Union 17

Bachli (Hughes' masseur) xii, 100, 101, 145, 148
Baltes, John 109, 110
Bancks, Jim 141
Barton, Edmund 28, 31
Baruch, Bernard 80
Bean, C.E.W. 57
Beazley, Kim (Snr) 67, 141
Beeby, George 19
Bellinger (tenant) xiv, 20–1, 109
Bennett, Gordon 139

Bernays, R.J. 119
Bevan, Aneurin 139
Birdwood, General William 71
Bjelke-Petersen, Joh 146
Booker, Malcolm 121
Borden, Robert 54
Botha, Louis 80
Brennan, Louis 150
Bright, John 2
British Labour Party 22
Brookes, George 3
Brosnan, Patrick xiv, 158
Browne, Frank 13
Bruce, Stanley 86, 87, 97, 112, 113, 115, 119, 120
Bumford, Frederick 19
Burdett, Francis 6

Calthorpe family 100, 132
Campbell, Mary Ann 44
Campbell, Mary, see Hughes, Mary (second wife)
Campbell, Thomas 44
Casey, Richard 147
Chamberlain, Neville 125, 134
Chifley, Ben 29
Churchill, Winston 79, 106, 139, 147
Clark, Manning xi
Clemenceau, Georges 76, 79, 80, 81, 123
Cock, John 22
Collins, Florrie 154

Communist Party of Australia   69, 115
conscription, see under Hughes, Billy
Cook, Joseph   20, 71, 72, 73, 75, 86
Cooper, Duff   139
Cotton, Frank   19
Country Party   86, 140
Coutts, Baroness Burdett   6, 7
Cowper, Norman   127, 128
Cripps, Stafford   22
Currie, George   151
Curtin, John   140, 141, 142, 143, 144
Cutts, Elizabeth (Hughes' first wife/
    de-facto partner) 14, 15, 25–6, 39,
    88, 91, 93, 109

Daley, C.S.   100, 101
Dash, George   138
Davies, Jane   121
Davies, Lord   125, 126
De Valera, Eamon   121
Deakin, Alfred   28, 31
Deane, Percy   5, 60, 71, 72, 76, 77, 81,
    83, 132, 139, 159
Deane, Shirley   159
Desmond, Jim   19
Dickens, Charles   6
Donald, W.H.   78
Ducker, Lyall   156
Duffy, Cyril   160
Duffy, David, see Hughes family,
    David
Dulles, John Foster   80

Edward I   41
Edward VIII   65, 129
Evans, Russell   15
Evatt, H.V.   30

Fadden, Arthur   48, 50, 129, 140, 143,
    147
Faisal, King   121
Farrell, John   19
Federation, see under Hughes, Billy

Fingleton, Jack   xiii
Fisher, Andrew   27, 30, 43, 44, 53, 54,
    57, 63, 69
Forde, Francis   122, 123
Fox, William   12

Garran, Robert   15, 71, 97, 100
George V   59
George, Henry   16
Gilmore, Mary   ix, 136, 148, 158
Givens, Tom   139
Green, Elizabeth   69
Green, Frank   94, 153
Grieve, Pauline   50
Gullett, Joe   116

Hagelthorn, F.W.   151
Haggard, Rider   55
Haig, General Douglas   67, 71
Haile Selassie   141
Hairgill, J.S.   7
Halifax, Lord   139
Hall, Daly   22
Hankey, Maurice   60, 77, 78
Hanlon, Edward   145
Hanson, Pauline   ix, 31
Harding, Warren   80
Hargrave, Lawrence   150
Harrowley, Lord   7
Haynes, Edith   155, 159, 160
Henderson, William   3
Henley, Thomas   124
Higgs, William   70
Hill, Billy   22
Hillyer, Ted   17
Hinkler, Bert   150
Hirohito, Emperor   76
Hitchin, Sam   22
Hitler, Adolf   125
Hobbs, Talbot   104
Holman, William   19, 20, 28, 30, 65,
    66, 70, 74, 75, 113, 115
Howard, John   ix

Index

Hughes, Billy (William Morris)
  ancestry 1–6
  awarded Companion of
     Honour 139
  birth 1, 5
  childhood 1–7, 33
  choice of Canberra as
     capital 98–102, 132
  death 13, 73, 155–61
  early employment 7, 11–19
  early political career 19–23, 25,
     28–30, 43
  family members, see Hughes family
  financial matters 47–9, 88–95, 132,
     146, 147, 147, 159–160
  first appointed Prime Minister 54,
     58–61
  health and hearing 102–7, 123, 128,
     130, 148, 149
  loss of Prime Ministerial role 85–7
  marriage 14, 26–7, 44–6
  mother's death 1, 5
  move to Australia 8–9, 11–12
  on conscription ix, 56, 63–74, 119,
     142, 158
  on Federation and states' rights 27,
     28, 53, 114
  on indigenous Australians 114
  on nationalism 63–74, 115
  on White Australia Policy and
     immigration ix, 31–2, 43, 113–14,
     128, 129
  oratory x, 8, 12, 15–18, 22, 29, 35,
     142, 154
  reckless driving 101–2, 128
  schooling 6–7
  secretaries xii–xiii, 51, 55, 60, 76,
     121, 123, 128, 140
  sexual matters 49–51
  sporting abilities 100, 102, 120
  trade union background 1, 15–18,
     30, 45
  Welsh background 33–42

World War I role 58–61, 63–74
World War II role 141–4
Hughes family (relationship to Billy
     Hughes in parentheses)
  Arthur (stepson) 14, 15, 25, 26, 58,
     94, 109, 126, 138, 147, 159
  Beryl (granddaughter) 109
  Bill, see Ernest
  Brian (nephew) 154
  Charles (son) 25, 27, 56, 57–8, 89,
     93, 95, 98, 109, 110, 111, 112, 113,
     116, 117, 118, 127, 137, 138, 146,
     147, 156, 159
  David (grandson) 160
  Dorothy, known as Dolly
     (daughter) 25, 27, 88, 91, 92, 93,
     94, 95, 112, 113, 135, 138, 147, 156,
     159
  Elizabeth (aunt) 4
  Elizabeth (first wife (or de-facto
     partner)) see Cutts, Elizabeth
  Ernest, known as Bill (son) 25, 27,
     55–7, 89, 93, 95, 109, 110, 116, 117,
     135, 147, 156, 159
  Ethel (daughter) 15, 25, 26, 27, 44,
     45, 56, 88–93, 95, 110, 127, 146,
     159
  Gwen (granddaughter) 126, 138
  Helen (daughter) 46, 54, 56, 59, 68,
     98, 101, 104, 110, 120, 131–7, 155,
     157, 159
  Hersee (daughter-in-law) 109
  Jane (mother) 1, 5
  Lily (daughter) 25, 27, 91, 92, 94,
     95, 111, 112, 117, 118, 127, 135,
     137, 138, 146, 147, 156, 159
  Mabel (daughter-in-law) 95, 126,
     138
  Maggie Hughes Gaskell
     (niece) 154
  Margaret (daughter-in-law) 111,
     117, 138, 147, 156
  Mary (aunt) 1, 33

Hughes family (*continued*)
   Mary (wife (or second wife)) xi, 35, 39, 44–6, 47, 48, 50, 54, 56, 69, 71, 86, 89, 94, 95, 97, 98, 100, 101, 104, 105, 116, 120, 127, 128, 132, 133, 134, 145, 147, 155, 156, 158, 159, 160
   Peter (uncle) 4
   Tudor Glyn (cousin) 156
   Wendy (relative on Cutts side of family) 109
   William (father) 1, 2, 6, 8
   William (grandson) 109, 116, 147
Hughes, Charles Evan (US politician) 80, 109
Hughes, Charles Evans (US Chief Justice) 126
Hughes, Richard (Welsh author) 38
Hungerford, Tom xii
Hunter, Percy 100

Imperial War Conference and Cabinet 73, 82
Iron Workers Union 141

Jenkins, Rachel 154
John, Augustus 72
Jones, Charles Lloyd 34, 35, 69
Jones, David 34
Jones, E.B. 81
Jones, Jack 55
Jones, Thomas 126
Jones, Ursula 51
Julius, George 150

Kelly, Ned xiii
Keynes, John Maynard 82
Kirkaldy, Reith 79

Labor Party, see Australian Labor Party
Labour Electoral League 16, 19, 20
Lamotte, Louis 19
Lan Yip, Henry 157
Lane, William 16

Lang, Jack 92, 107
Lang, John Dunmore 27
Larwood, Harold xiii
Latham, John 71, 72
Laurie, Bill ix
Law, Bonar 64, 77, 78
Lawrence, T.E. 121
League of Nations 75, 76, 77, 83, 120, 123, 124, 125
Levy, Pat 135
Liberal Party (Australia), see also United Australia Party 69, 144, 147
Liberals (UK) 102
Lloyd George, David 1, 33, 37, 38, 39–42, 55, 57, 59, 60, 64, 65, 76, 77, 78, 83, 86, 102, 123, 135, 139
Lloyd, John xiii
Lloyd, Lady Frances 41
Lloyd, Owen 107
Lowe, Beth 138, 146
Lyons, Enid 59, 122, 123, 129, 130, 147, 148
Lyons, Joseph 120, 122, 123, 124, 125, 135, 136, 138, 139

Macarthur, General George 143
MacDonald, Malcolm 135
Macdonald, Ramsay 22
Mackinnon, Colin 151
Mahomed, Dorothy 121–2, 137
Mahon, Hugh 70
Mahoney, Bill 17
Mailey, Arthur 141
Makino, Baron 75, 76
Mannix, Archbishop David 65–6, 135, 137
Marks, Walter 19
Mary, Queen (wife of George V) 59
Massey, William 54
McCristal, T.W. 18, 158
McEwen, John 'Black Jack' 147, 148
McGrath, J.J. 21
McLellan, Elizabeth 26

Index

McMahon, William 147
Menzies, Robert 121, 123, 129, 135, 138, 139, 147
Monash, John 57, 71
Morisson, Herbert 139
Morris, Mary 1
Morris, Peter 1
Mort, I.S. 150
Mubarak, Hosni 161
Mungo-Ferguson, Ronald x
Murdoch, Elizabeth 69, 125
Murdoch, Keith 20, 57, 59, 60, 61, 64, 67, 68, 69, 70, 71, 75, 113, 124, 125, 135
Mussolini, Benito 113, 141

Nationalist Party, also known as National Party 86, 113, 115, 120
Nicholas, George 47
Nichols, Marjorie 51
Northam, Olga 51
Northcliffe, Lord 58

O'Brien, T.J. 59
Oakes, Charlie 19
Orlando, Vittorio 77

Paderewski, Ignace 81
Page, Earle 73, 86, 113, 135, 147
Pal, Justice 76
Pankhurst, Adela 69
Pankhurst, Emmeline 69
Paris Peace Conference, see also Versailles Treaty ix, x, 38, 46, 75–83, 99, 106, 121, 128
Parkes, Henry 15, 22, 28
Payne, Fred 13
Payne, George 8, 11, 159
Peace Conference, see Paris Peace Conference
Pearce, George 57, 60, 86, 87
Pilter, Charlie 19
Price, Ivie 36, 50

Reid, George 28
Richards, Henry 16
Riddell, Lord 59
Ridge, Eddie 3
Ridge, Johnnie 3
Rignold, George 15
Roberts, George 3
Roberts, Tom 22, 139
Robinson, W.S. 54, 60
Rogers, Barbara xii
Romans, Pat xii
Routley, Tom 19
Ryan, T.J. xiv, 70
Ryrie, Granville de Lane 18

Scott, Walter 26
Scullin, James 119, 120
Seamen's Union 69
Shepherd (secretary) 55
Short, R.W. 27
Smith, Keith 150
Smith, Ross 150
Smuts, Jan 81
Snodgrass, Viti 49
Solidarity Party 43
Sonnino, Sidney 81
Spence, William Guthrie 17
Spender, Percy 147
Stanley, Arthur Penrhyn 8
Stewart, Margaret 27
Storey, David 19
Streeton, Arthur 104, 105, 139
Sullivan, 'Sully' 18
Sulman, John 98
Sydney, Arthur 141

Thatcher, Margaret 81
Tillett, Ben 22, 127, 155
Toohey, W.J. 65
Torrington, Enid Beary 36
Tracey, R.J. 102
Transport Workers Federation 17

Trolly, Draymen and Carters Union 17
Tudor, Frank 70
Turnbull, Harry 19
Turton, Willard 21

United Australia Party, see also Liberal Party 120, 127, 140, 144

Versailles Treaty, see also Paris Peace Conference ix, 80
Villiers, Charles xii

Wade (Nationalist Party founder) 115
Wakefield, Lord 133, 134, 135
Walker, George 19
Waller, Keith xiii
Walsh, Tom 69
Waterside Workers Federation 17, 19, 30, 73–4, 103, 141

Watson, J.C. 20, 23, 25, 29
Watt, William 82
West, Morris xiii
Whaley, F.S. 47
Wharf Labourers Union 17, 73, 158
White Australia Policy, see under Hughes, Billy
Whitlam, Gough ix
Whitney, Winifred 154
Williams, Diana 26, 109, 116
Williams, Ernest 26
Williams, R. 38
Wilson, Woodrow 37, 46, 71, 76, 77, 78, 80, 81, 82, 106, 126
Wingate, Ronald 81
World War I ix, 53–4, 57, 58–61, 64–74
World War II x, 141–4

Yewen, A.G. 19